One More Shot

Hormones, Heartbreak & Humor
Surviving IVF at 40-ish!

One More Shot

Hormones, Heartbreak & Humor
Surviving IVF at 40-ish!

Mandy M. Refvik

ISBN: 9798990796508 (Print)
ISBN: 9798990796515 (E-book)
ISBN: 9798990796522 (Audiobook)

Library of Congress Control Number: 2024912798

Printed in the United States of America.

https://www.mandyrefvik.com

First Edition

Dedication

To those who dare to dream, persevere through challenges, and find strength in vulnerability.
May this book inspire you and light the path of your own journey.

To my beloved daughter, my greatest treasure.
You are a testament to the strength and beauty that arise from life's most challenging journeys.
You are the very heartbeat of this book.

In moments of crisis, unseen but near,
A little girl's smile, calming all fear.
From steering wheel's impact to wedding's bright day,
She played in silence, guiding my way.

Underwater depths, a glimpse of her grace,
Swimming beside me, in that peaceful space.
Then came the moment, my baby's first cry,
Her face mirroring hers, I knew why.

A connection unspoken, a bond so real,
In her eyes, the little girl's smile I feel.
Through trials and triumphs, she's always been there,
My guardian angel, beyond compare.

Table of Contents

Preface

Traveling Companions

If you've picked up this book, it's most likely that you or someone you love is considering fertility treatments and you're hoping that someone with real life experience can help you learn more to better weigh your options. That's exactly the kind of help I hope to be for you, and why I wrote this book. Because when *I* was first going through it all, I would have loved to have found a resource exactly like this one, written by someone who truly gets it.

But first, let me be clear. I'm not a medical professional, and I don't play one on TV! The stats that I will share with you can all easily be found online (only they will be gathered here in one place for you). This isn't a how-to, or an article for *Scientific American*. It's the story of one woman's personal journey through fertility treatments—what she learned, the choices (including the mistakes) she made, and how it all affected her and her loved ones.

I will share the good, the bad, and the ugly—as well as the sucky, the embarrassing, the joyful, and the beautiful. I will be honest with you in the following pages—no sugar-coating allowed. So, get ready to read those F-bombs when I share what it was like to be super-hormonal! But I also hope to be supportive—no judgments allowed either! We all enter our journeys through different lanes, but now we're all in this together—maybe even stuck in the same traffic jam!

I hope that you consider the moments you spend reading these chapters to be like an afternoon's intimate conversation with a close girlfriend who is sharing her story with you over coffee (or tea, or a glass of wine). Ultimately, I am here bearing my soul so that you don't feel alone on the road less traveled to having a baby. Because I promise you, no matter what crazy thoughts have entered your head or what feelings you are trying to process, you are not alone!

I can't think of a better travel companion than you!

Prologue

A Vision

A clock! For my whole life, I've been racing against time. And I was always late—late for work, late for meetings, late in my career, late with my period, late with starting a family—late, late, late! But that's life for me. The universe provided, in its way, but never completely. Little did I know in my twenties that every experience and challenge was merely a learning tool (wouldn't it be nice to know that in our twenties?). It wasn't until I was getting closer to my forties that things began to make more sense.

I viewed my life after college in one specific way. I was going to have an exhilarating career in movie production. I would become a director of a ton of major films with a celebrity husband on my arm, all while traveling around the world. Although my plans included a husband (a celebrity husband at that), children didn't factor into my preconceived family. Why, you ask? *Hmm,* I think it's because when I started my career in the film industry and made the decision to move to Hollywood, I noticed that every woman who had a position behind the scenes and who decided to move up in her career didn't have children. It seemed like the norm. I would hear them say, "You must be shoulder to shoulder with men, and you cannot appear weak or emotional and caring for children will not give you the time to do your job." I listened ... and I believed them.

I know those reading this book now will say, "Of course, we can do it all, including children! Women do it every single day!" And I agree 100% *today*. But then, in the early 2000s, most companies still looked at women as unqualified for the coveted positions of producer and director ... and we knew it. The successful businesswoman persona can be challenged at every seam, including adding children to the mix.

At that time, the work environment was predominately male. Men ran the war room in the newsroom. Men were on cameras because "dainty hands couldn't hold a camera properly." Women should only be in front of the camera, look pretty, and listen to what they are told to do.

The men in the room would consistently speak down to the female producers and directors even if their positions were below theirs. And this was what I saw and to keep a position of power, women had to be aggressive, ruthless, and a little bit selfish. This was my current dream, so I followed suit.

While working in Hollywood might seem like a great overnight success for some, for me, it became a challenge. My move from New York, NY to Los Angeles, Ca. after film school led me to take any production job that was presented (and I mean any!). Big opportunities were not dropped on your lap, you had to work hard for it, and it took a lot of time and meeting that celebrity husband took even longer.

One day I was set to shoot on multiple locations where we would set up, shoot, hide from cops, check off our shot list, load equipment back into vehicle, and then head to the next scene as soon as possible. The list consisted of scenery of swaying palm trees, moving cars, and people walking by. After a few hours, a coworker who'd also been on set with me said he would join me for lunch, and he would help me take the rest of the equipment to the next location which was about 25 minutes away. We had enjoyed a quick bite together and had been aware that we were racing against the clock.

Story of my life! Unfortunately (but not surprisingly), we found ourselves stuck in traffic—wonderful Los Angeles traffic! We made small talk, listened to music, and tried not to rage at the other drivers. Then, as my coworker announced (again) how we were running late—WHAM!

The last thing I recalled was a ringing in my ear, a loud screeching sound that gradually faded to a low hum. As I looked around, everything felt strange and unfamiliar. The sound persisted, and I couldn't pinpoint its origin. As I rubbed my forehead, a sharp pain surged through me. My vision was blurry, and I struggled to gain clarity.

Then out of nowhere, a little girl appeared before me. She had the most beautiful brown eyes, framed by the longest eyelashes I had ever seen, and a head of soft light brown curls. I reached out to her, and she touched my hand. Without words, she nodded yes. She smiled at me with the softest smile, offering a recognition and assurance that felt oddly comforting.

Yet, I couldn't shake the questions swirling in my mind. *Who was this child? Why was she looking at me with such familiarity?* I was mesmerized by her presence, unable to look away or communicate with her. *Was she hurt?*

She seemed unscathed. Suddenly, I noticed throbbing pain again and closed my eyes. Amidst the haze, I heard a distant voice calling out to me and just like that I was back to reality and feeling very unfamiliar.

"Mandy! Mandy! Are you okay? Mandy!"

My coworker's voice filtered through my right ear, and just like that, I was back in my car in the middle of the highway. Overhearing horns honking in time to the throbbing of my forehead. *What had happened? Where was that little girl?*

Witnesses later explained to me that we'd been rear-ended. The sudden force from behind slammed my car into the truck in front of me, which made me hit my head on the steering wheel, and then…apparently imagined a little girl. Sounds like a Hollywood film, doesn't it?

But it wasn't, and I was back to racing time.

This was my fucking life!

Chapter 1

Threads of Change

My dreams of 'making it big' fueled my passion to live in Los Angeles, CA. Most of the friends I had made in college remained in New York to work and play, and I always made it a point to visit my family and friends as much as I could. I missed them. One trip back home was not for what most would consider a 'major' holiday, but for many New Yorkers, it is. I flew in the week of the big St. Paddy's Day grand parade. When I arrived in New York City that evening, I expected to follow my usual M.O. of going straight to my parents' place from the airport, but this time, it was decided by my friends that they would pick me up and we would go straight to the parties that were happening in New York City.

"You can spend time with your family later," they told me. "This time, we see you first! And we're going out!" my friend yelled over the phone.

It took little to no convincing. I was ready to have a good time and blow off steam after a hectic work week. My flight arrived on time and a car loaded with four girls arrived for a pickup on time as well. Dressed and ready to go out. This was happening. So, I loaded my luggage into the car, hopped in, and began freshening up my makeup in the rear-view mirror. We chatted and laughed without missing a beat. That's one of the best things about having old friends. You can spend long stretches of time apart, and then the moment you're reunited, you pick up right where you left off. This is why I always made it a point to visit with them during the holidays or whenever I could afford a ticket. It's just easy! There is no awkward warmup period like with others—it's a straight dive into laughter and good times. And that's what I was looking forward to when we rolled up to the club—a fun weekend with my girlfriends.

As we entered the club, I let the beat of the music wash over me. I walked up to the bar and ordered a drink while swaying to the music. A couple of drinks later, okay, maybe a lot of drinks later, a guy tapped me on the shoulder. I'd never seen him before. He was clutching a pint of beer and seemed already wasted. By then, I was buzzing myself, basking in the glow of several drinks. I was feeling relaxed and at home … and happy.

"Hi," he shouted over the music and leaned in a little. "I'm Johnnie!"

"Hi," I said back, but thought, *Johnnie… Johnnie… Where had I heard that name before?* My brain was a little fuzzy, but it finally clicked. *Johnnie!*

"Oh! I've heard so much about you."

"Yeah, same here," he said and smiled.

As it turns out, I had heard a lot about this guy before. In fact, there had been a ton of build-up about him, and then we just coincidentally meet—very anticlimactic! Still, I couldn't help but laugh that it had finally happened, and my friend could shut up about it!

"Mandy, you've got to meet him," my friend said with a mischievous kind of sparkle in her eye. "His name is Johnnie. He's so fun—and fun*ny*. And I just knew immediately you two would hit it off."

"Are you really trying to set me up?" I couldn't believe it. It was like she forgot that I didn't live in New York anymore.

I was also a little offended that she thought I needed setting up—like my dating life wasn't going well in Los Angeles or something. Truthfully, it *wasn't* anything to brag about, but set-ups just weren't for me. They seemed a little too reality-TV-show-meets-Hallmark-holiday-movie for my blood. And neither described my life.

"And so, we finally meet," I said.

He smiled.

We didn't say much else. Maybe it was because the music was so loud it made it hard to talk, or maybe because we'd both had a lot to drink, but we went our separate ways at the end of the night. We didn't exchange anything but pleasantries that night. But it didn't matter. It had taken us so long to meet as it was that I doubted we'd manage to cross paths again anytime soon. Interestingly enough, I did meet an Irishman on Saint Patricks Day.

My trip was fun filled, but then it was time to get back to Los Angeles. A few days later, I got a ding on my Myspace account—the original social media platform (and no need to do the math—I am over 40). The ding was an alert that you had a message. I was excited to see who messaged me, and saw it was from Johnnie. He said it was nice to meet me and that hopefully we could meet again soon. Well, lucky for him, soon was not too far away. I would have to return to New York a few months later for a college friend's wedding. And, as fate would have it, my college friend was marrying Johnnie's business partner.

This wedding location would be in New Jersey. My friend suggested that she would drive. "I will swing by and pick up Johnnie and then head your way," she said.

The name didn't ring a bell again, "Johnnie." As they pulled up to the front of my parent's house, the same Irishman I met at the bar months ago came out of the car to open the door for me like a gentleman. In the car, I got to know a lot more about Johnnie, his family, his friends, and who he was as a person. We laughed a lot, mostly at each other, which was nice to experience. He was okay at laughing at himself and his quirks. As much as we talked, we still didn't exchange phone numbers, but he did have my Myspace name. It wasn't like I wasn't interested; it just seemed like my place was in Los Angeles and his was New York and it didn't make sense for either of us. The wedding was a beautiful event for our friends, and a perfect place for catch up. But then it would be back to Los Angeles.

My next trip wouldn't be long after, in October of that year, and for another beautiful occasion. My family of seven (three younger brothers, both parents, a sister-in-law, and me) recently became eight when my brother Robin and his wife Lynette had a beautiful baby girl. So, it was back to New York for the family-filled, joyous christening of my first niece. However, for my family, this happiness would soon be followed by utter heartbreak.

Three days later after the celebration, my mom sat me down to tell me that she went to her doctor, and they diagnosed her with cancer.

"Breast cancer," she specified. Then she burst into tears before whispering, "Stage 2."

What? For a few seconds I couldn't comprehend what she was saying. When I did, all I could think was *Fuck!* My brain screamed. *Cancer!* And then: *Fuck cancer!*

How dare this disease touch my mother? I was in shock. My only instinct was to scream from the top of my lungs. But I held back. I had to, for her.

As I came out of my otherworldly state, questions came tumbling out—

"Do you know what stage it is?"

"Yes. Stage 2," she exclaimed and looked at me as if to say, "I just told you so."

"Are you going to have chemo?"

"I don't know!"

"What exactly did the doctor say?"

"I can't remember."

My mom shook her head in confusion. She was unable to string words together coherently between her sobs. She couldn't remember much of what the doctor said after he gave her the terrifying diagnosis. She didn't know what she would do, and I didn't know what I would do. I didn't know the first thing about cancer or treatment. How could I console her? Until then, there had been no cancer in our family. The only thing I knew was that I wanted and had to support her as best as possible. I had to fix this. But how?

The past few months before this revelation, I had been totally disconnected from my mom. And I never felt more guilty or ashamed than I did in that moment. I thought everything was good. I was consumed with my life in Los Angeles and coming back and forth to New York for partying and celebration after celebration, but this whole time I was clueless about what mattered most—my mom's health.

In my head, the answer rang loud and clear—I needed to stay in New York and be there for her. This nagging feeling that I felt inside urged me to change my life around and be available to her. I would leave my first big gig in Hollywood and the circle of friends I made. This decision was made from pain and guilt. But regardless of how I decided to leave everything in the drop of a dime. It was the most important thing that had to be done. And I felt in my heart I could do it.

I slept on my mom's living room couch and made myself comfy with my laptop. I Googled, "What is cancer?" "What do you do about cancer?" "What should you eat?", etc. I talked to my mom more about what the doctor had said to her and asked that we go back together to speak to the doctor. I wanted to be there to hear exactly what the results of her labs were and to understand what my next steps would be to assist her.

I isolated myself from everyone in my life in Los Angeles and New York, by focusing too intently. I found myself becoming scared, sad, and helpless. Days went by and I lived in pjs and my hair in a bun in front of a laptop. I would only dress to go to doctors' appointments.

I turned my mother's kitchen into a smoothie shop, where I was offering her a new type of smoothie or juice to help strengthen her body as much as possible. After finally getting a third opinion and confirmation that her cancer was Stage 2, we found out she would need to have a mastectomy on the left and a lumpectomy on the right.

Our days were stressful. Our family walked around the house in silence, not knowing what to say or do. We played board games in the evenings, and we sat around laughing and joking with my mom. One day I just needed to get away from the Googling of cancer and doctor's appointments.

I decided to log into my Myspace account. It had been two months since I had talked to anyone. I saw that Johnnie had sent me a few messages (he had clearly seen from pictures I had previously posted that I was still in New York), but they had been sitting there ignored, along with messages from friends. Having basic conversations seemed meaningless.

Ding!

Another message popped up.

"Would you be up for a drink tonight?"

"Not feeling up to it. Going through some stuff," was my first response in the six messages that were left.

"Can I ask what?"

Somehow, that one question unlocked the floodgates. So much for not wanting to talk! I took a deep breath and began banging away on my laptop. *Seriously, what just happened? I barely know this guy!* I expected him to ghost me—and I wouldn't have blamed him—way too much, too soon. It was a heavy subject to bring up with someone I barely knew. And on a chat. I was sure he'd double think that drink offer. I think at the time, I just needed to speak with someone—anyone—and I hadn't realized it until then.

His response surprised me, though.

"Come out for an hour. Have a drink with me. It'll do you good to step away from it for a bit."

I did need a break! So, I agreed (although a little reluctantly) and made plans to meet up with him that evening.

As I got ready, I began having second thoughts. By the time I was standing under the warm shower, doubt after doubt cascaded over me along with the water. *What am I doing? This is crazy. I don't want to talk to anyone right now. I have too much to deal with!* And I convinced myself to cancel our date as soon as I got out of the shower.

But as I toweled off, I talked myself back into it. I didn't need to feel guilty for taking a little time out. I will be back with my mom soon. She would be okay if I was out for a couple of hours. Plus, there was this dress I had packed for this trip but hadn't worn yet. Maybe it could use a night out, too.

Once I was all dressed up and ready to go, I found myself wanting to cancel again! But I willed my legs to carry me out of the house and down to the subway, where I found the MTA subway delayed... how relatable. Clenching my jaw, I fished my phone out of my purse to call Johnnie and tell him I would be late. But the screen was dark. My phone was dead. *Of course, it was.*

As the train arrived, I stepped in with a loud sigh, sat down, and once again questioned if I should bother. Had my mom not been sick, this would never have even been a debate in my head. I was usually up for going out. But these guilt-ridden thoughts plummeted my mind. *Why did I leave her for this date? What was she thinking right now? How was she feeling?*

Our meeting point was a very quaint restaurant called Dos Caminos restaurant in SoHo. By the time I arrived, I was an hour late. I figured there was no way he was still there. But I thought well, I tried, which felt like "enough" to me. I walked in, expecting to turn around and immediately walk back out again.

But there he was, looking handsome and happy to see me. He smiled and waved me over, seeming really excited I was there.

We sat, we ate, and we talked. Then, after dinner, we walked around the city and talked even more. So, yeah, we took longer than he suggested especially considering I had already been an hour late.

It was the break from "real life" I didn't know I needed. His humor and patience gave me comfort, peace, and strength. And after that very special date, we began seeing each other regularly—for coffee, lunch, dinner, wine, or even just a walk. It felt good. He felt good. No matter where I was on my emotional rollercoaster, he was steady and strong. He was just the shoulder I needed to lean on.

Ironically, after Johnnie and I met at Dos Caminos and then began a relationship, I learned that the phrase "Dos Caminos" means two ways (paths, roads, or journeys). It hit me that as I was learning to manage my anger, frustration, and petrified emotions with my mom's cancer diagnosis, I was also managing another path that was filled with the excitement, happiness, and hopeful emotions of a new relationship. Because of this second path, I was starting to feel some comfort in everything going on around me. Our relationship started to bloom and as an added, but unexpected, bonus, my support for my mom became easier to manage. My head was much clearer walking into the doctor's office and even in my research.

As life would have it, fucking cancer reared its ugly head in another way. Just as Johnnie and I were beginning to navigate our new relationship, and my mom was dealing with her healing process after the mastectomy and treatment, Johnnie's mother was diagnosed with Stage 3 ovarian cancer.

Now it was my turn to be that shoulder for Johnnie and offer what he gave me when I first found out about cancer. We found ourselves each taking our respective Moms to their appointments—sometimes, on the same days—and texting each other from waiting rooms across town.

We'd then get on the phone and give each other a full report on our moms' conditions and how we felt about it.

As devastating as it was for both of us, it was also so comforting to have someone to unload on—someone we could be honest with and even cry in front of, but also who understood exactly what we were going through. We each became the other's best friend, confidant, and screaming box within a short amount of time. The bond we created out of love and worry for our moms was irreplaceable.

The very thing I was most afraid of happening to me happened to him. After three months in the hospital, his mom passed away. Johnnie lost the most important person in his life. She had been his world, which was now upside down in the worst conceivable way.

Based on his demeanour and nature, you could see the Mom she was, although I sadly never got to meet her. She was a soul who could easily draw others to herself with her calm, accepting, and warm presence. Known affectionately as Margie, she had been a resilient woman who approached life with fierce love and determination. Throughout her illness, Margie remained a beacon of hope and positivity. She saw life as a celebration, especially in raising her two sons to be compassionate and well-rounded individuals. She succeeded beyond measure.

As much as I wanted to help fix this, I couldn't. I didn't know what to do, what to say, or even how to be. And for a long time afterward, it was as if the light had left him. Evenings were especially hard, as we didn't really talk much. We weren't living together yet, but there were many sleepovers. This one evening, after a quick dinner, Johnnie just wanted to go to bed early. It had been a few days after the funeral, and he was still in a sad place. We both climbed into bed with a quick goodnight kiss, and fell right asleep, our bodies and minds in clear need of a rest.

At about 1:00 AM, my eyes flew open to see this shape hovering over the foot of the bed. I remember vividly not feeling scared but trying to figure out if I knew this silhouette. It just felt familiar.

All I remember was the movement was slow through the air. I felt something but didn't see a face or arms or legs. I was lying on my back, my eyes open, and nothing else moved, just my eyes. I watched the shape slowly move to the left side of the bed, where Johnnie was sleeping.

It was as if it spoke.

Not knowing exactly how to respond to this unexpected visit and message, I found myself nodding, as if to say "Okay."

Then, I glanced over to Johnnie's side of the bed. His eyes were open as well, and he was looking directly at the silhouette too. He seemed to be seeing what I was seeing!

He nodded, "Okay."

I recalled a sense of comfort afterward and enjoyed the deepest and most refreshing sleep I've ever had in months.

The following morning, Johnnie and I drifted around the house, both much more silent than usual. It was clear that neither of us wanted to bring up the night before. I know I wanted to make sense of what I thought I had seen and why I had seen it. *Was it a dream? Did I make it up?*

I blurted it out over coffee in my own distinctive Mandy style, "Was I dreaming, or were you staring at the wall last night?" I asked.

Johnnie seemed relieved at the invitation to speak. He asked excitedly, "Did you see her? She looked like my mom!"

I intern couldn't figure what it was for me. But if it were mama Margie, her presence did offer him some peace, but it would be a long time before Johnnie was Johnnie again. He was saddened for years over this loss. And I did the best I could to be there for him, all the while praying I wouldn't be going through something similar.

I'm no therapist, but I feel they would clearly call this type of relationship "trauma bonding." It is a type of bonding that occurs because of the intense emotional experiences that come from coping with traumatic events. There is power when you're experiencing such raw emotions at the exact same time and can be that vulnerable with each other.

Interestingly, our moms and their loving motherhood bonded us beyond our worry and grief. The very idea of motherhood, and specifically, my desire to be a mother to a child as our mothers had/have been to us, would bond us even more. Something I didn't realize until much later.

Chapter 2

The Famous F Word

Despite all that we were going through personally, Johnnie and I took comfort in each other and in building our relationship. Not long after, the great 2003 recession emerged, a crisis that sent shock waves around the world. When the stock market crashed, it only further compounded an already dire situation. It was a difficult time for Johnnie and his company, facing an unexpected roadblock that necessitated employee downsizing. As for me, I found myself out of work and grappling with the harsh realities of the economic downturn. Like so many others, Johnnie and I were forced to take whatever work we could find as we weathered the seemingly never-ending storm.

Luckily, Johnnie got an opportunity to contract himself out to work in Southern California to keep his company afloat. This felt like the chance for me to get back to my life in Los Angeles and work in production. And a place for Johnnie to have a fresh start. Palm trees and sunshine could provide a soothing presence and would offer a touch of serenity to his soul. We were both ready for a change, and this had come at the right time. We packed our lives up into a storage unit with the belief that we would be back to New York soon. My mom was in remission—she was back at work and feeling great, much to my relief.

We rented a small house on a cliff with a view of the ocean—it was a fully furnished home. This made sense because all we had were the clothes we travelled with. These two New Yorkers had enough sorrow to last a lifetime. We somehow felt freer and more at ease, and we got to explore our relationship with a lens that wasn't clouded with despair.

We spent a lot of time with each other and bonded in different ways than we had in New York. It was here where we fell deeply in love, free to just be ourselves. With all the fun in the California sun, time had passed, and before I knew it, we had celebrated five years of dating bliss! Johnnie and I had a good thing going. My mom was still in remission, and Johnnie was slowly healing.

One day, we were getting together with one of Johnnie's college buddies and his wife. They had flown in from New York, and in their efforts to meet up with as many friends as possible in the limited window they had, they asked if they could bring along another couple to join us. I had no idea when I agreed that this lunch would be a truly clear indication of my obliviousness when it came to my maternal clock. In fact, I don't think I had ever thought of the term "maternal clock," let alone said it out loud. *Who knew that had to be checked?* So, yes, on one blissful sunny California day, I became quickly overwhelmed by information I didn't know I was missing!

We met at an outdoor restaurant with a gorgeous ocean view. Johnnie and his friend dove immediately into joking, laughing, and remembering the "good ol' days," like it was fifteen years earlier and included the additional husband into the banter. This left me trying to find a connection with the wives, neither of whom I had ever met before. Since I can be a little shy when first meeting people, the initial "getting to know you" stage can be awkward for me. So, trying to get a conversation going, I noticed the obvious pregnant belly of the friend's friend and said, "Congratulations!"

The woman from the other couple who was with us joined in. "Yes, I am so happy for you. I know you have been trying for a while!"

The pregnant woman beamed. "Thank you!" And then, to my surprise, she launched straight into her "How I Got Pregnant" story.

We had all just met, and now I am about to hear all the tidbits of how her and her husband worked on having a baby. Something I was not really interested in at first. She shared that she and her husband had struggled to get pregnant and tried many techniques and treatments … to no avail. Then she went into how frustrated and disappointed they had been until, she excitedly proclaimed, "We found this brilliant doctor, and we did IVF!"

As I stared at her like a deer in headlights, a half grin on my face, not wanting to show that I did not know what she meant, my brain scrambled to make sense of the three letters she said aloud (and with such passion).

Did the "IV" part mean "in the vagina"? If so, what word did the "F" part stand for? Not... that "F" word... right? Nah, it couldn't be! That was the usual way to make a baby, but she was talking about a different way, so... wait, what was she talking about?

I kept my thoughts to myself (thankfully!), not wanting to ask questions that exposed my ignorance. I was already feeling so uncomfortable, and this conversation was the icing on the cake. I pushed my salad around with my fork, pretending to be more distracted by tomatoes than this conversation, and wishing they would change the subject. *Why did I have to notice the elephant in the room and bring up pregnancy? Ugh!*

Then, the inevitable question. The pregnant woman looked over at me and asked, "Do you have kids?"

I answered with a head shake, no. Then she asked the ultimate follow up, "Are you going to have children?"

My answer then was a smile and a head tilt, yes. I don't know why I said that because I really didn't know. I think I was just going with the flow of the conversation.

When lunch was over, we all said our goodbyes and that was that. I never saw those women again. But that conversation left an impression on me because, after that lunch, I thought about it.

Why didn't I know what this letter F in the IVF word is?

I thought about the F. The F word. And decided I had to Google it out of curiosity. And before I knew it, I went down a rabbit hole like none other ... all with the F word.

F for Family, F for Fruitfulness, F for Feminine, F for Fertility, F for Fertile Window, F for Fertile Myrtle, F for Flow, F for Fuck, and F for Fertility Rate.

So, I learned I was wrong about the IV, it was NOT "in the vagina," as I had assumed. And I was completely off on the F as well.

The F, *Oh! the F is for Fertilization. Ha! I am a complete Fucking idiot! In Vitro Fertilization (IVF)*

Why hadn't I ever thought about my fertility before? Did I know that something was not right deep down? Or was I blissfully ignorant of the next F word for Family?

And now that I had gone down the hole, I just kept digging deeper into my thoughts ... Why hadn't we ever gotten pregnant in all these years? We'd never even once had a scare. Not that we would have considered pregnancy a "scare." But we had stopped using contraception a long time ago. Although we were not yet married and living together it would have just made sense for it to happen.

But it's not like we were purposely not seeking to have children, either....

Let's see... We had sex. I got my period. We had sex. I got my period. We had sex. I got my period...

The repetition began sounding like the chorus of a Cardi B rap song. Having sex was not an issue or problem for us. We enjoyed it in romantic ways and in most of the kinkiest ways. I mean, we didn't get into bondage, *per se*, but we may have used some cheap handcuffs from time to time. *Sorry, Mom!*

Now, new questions began to creep into my mind and started leaving empty holes ... *Were we really trying? Does Johnnie even want kids? Do I? Why had we never even really talked about it? Was I afraid of the answers?*

This last question blew me away.

One night, not long after I entered the rabbit hole, I asked Johnnie, *"Have you ever thought about us having kids?"*

Johnnie turned to look at me with a blank stare. *"I've ... thought about it,"* he admitted, *"but since you never brought it up, I figured we were good where we're at."*

18

In a deep sigh. I nodded to myself. *We are good! We're great, in fact!* Yet, I suddenly felt a weird urge in my belly that I had never felt before as I walked away.

But Johnnie's answer still didn't explain why. *Why hadn't we gotten pregnant in five years of being together and without using contraception?* Something about that just wasn't sitting well with me.

So, suddenly the F in my story had an entirely different meaning. It meant FAILED. I Failed. But I wasn't sure how … yet.

Chapter 3

'Chance' Encounter

After several weeks of trying to convince myself that our life was good and that we had a good thing going and I didn't need anything else, I gave into the million-dollar question, within my mind, a million-dollar answer. I believed we hadn't gotten pregnant because we hadn't been intentional. *That had to be it!* With all the shit out there about visualization, and "The Secret," and affirmations, of course that had to be it! I had never once envisioned a baby. I hadn't thought about it at all. Well, that shit was going to change right then and there.

After a few days of digesting all of Google's information and fulfilling my need to be intentional, I sat Johnnie down and told him how I felt. I told him that I had a nagging feeling that we needed to really start working on a family. We talked and talked and talked. It was as if I had to have answers not only to all my why's and how's, but then all his. Like how will we afford children with our current financial state? How will we continue our lifestyle if we have children?

"Babe, you know those little rugrats are always sick. We will always be sick. Are you ready for that?"

After long debates back and forth, he was semi onboard, and that was good enough for me. And from now on I … I mean WE … were going to be as deliberate as possible. And it was time to get busy! We were, or *I was*, making a mutha f*ckn baby! Thankfully, Johnnie went right along with my intentions. I mean, you usually don't have to convince men you want to have *more* sex!

He was onboard! But he also seemed silently curious as well.

We worked on conceiving on every surface of our home. It was fun, but for months we only ended up with some questionable stains and a lot of disappointment. At first, trying to conceive was like a thrilling adventure. So much to see, so much to do. We were even getting it done during our lunch breaks, multi-tasking like bosses and sometimes while watching Grey's Anatomy.

Ovulation calendars and sticky notes were everywhere, like a crime scene investigation board on our bedroom wall. I was trying to find the missing baby I didn't know existed a few months ago. But all we found were negative pregnancy tests. In keeping with a positive mindset, I would even take one if I was a day late, in hopes that this would be the month. But I kept coming up blank. I needed positive results. I was very analytical about the whole thing, like a detective trying to solve a cold case. I was on a mission and needed to succeed. Period (no pun intended).

Before I knew it, an entire year had passed, and nada, zip, zilch.

To make matters worse, all I saw was one of two things—babies or pregnant women. And on special days, I saw them both ... everywhere. I was beginning to feel jealous and angry. All I wanted to do was throw up, and it wasn't from being pregnant.

A very friendly woman told me one day that what I was experiencing was what the rest of the world called "baby season." It's in spring and for whatever that means, everyone else got the memo to get pregnant around that time, so they can show up at Christmas dinners with baby in hand. *Oh, what fun!* Then, there is the "baby storm" filled with baby announcements, showers, and kids' birthday parties .... for everyone but us. It felt like everyone was able to get pregnant so easily.

All while attending these events to support friends and family, there always came the whispers and questions—*When are you having a baby?* I tried so hard to be polite, but seriously, after about a million times being asked when we would spawn our "mini-mes," I was so tired of it. I couldn't take it anymore. Dodging these nosy, know-nothings was impossible, like trying to avoid a swarm of mosquitoes on a summer night.

They were everywhere—the store, the bank, walking in the park, and the most frequent were in our own circle! When I slipped up and let the cat out of the bag about our little fertility struggles, thinking it would make them lay off a bit, it only made things one hundred times worse. Everyone became a fertility expert! People were ready to whip out their unsolicited advice like an expired coupon, just begging someone to accept it.

The onslaught of emotions I was beginning to experience at these events, or any time the subject was brought up, stirred up a lot of stuff I didn't know was there. I am a very logical and analytical person, not an emotional basket case. So, *why was I getting so upset?* I know they weren't trying to hurt me. But I soon found that my emotions were in the driver's seat, kicking all my rational thinking right out the damn window. The uneasiness inside was escalating with every question they asked—every answer I couldn't give. Not to mention, my RBF (resting bitch face) wasn't always the most helpful when it came to answering questions. And let's say my smart-ass mouth wasn't an angel either.

"You just need to relax! Go, on a vacation, like to a tropical island!"

My response: *Oh sure, 'relax' and take a tropical vacation, easy peasy! Hey, while you're at it, why don't ya whip out that check book and book me two first-class tickets to paradise? Thanks! I will start packing now.*

"Try acupuncture!"

My thoughts—*I'm not into needles!* (Little did I know how much this would come back to bite me!)

"Do goat yoga!"

My response: *I'm not into animals touching me!*

"Sitting in front of electronics makes you infertile. Have you tried blue light glasses?

My thoughts: *Does my uterus have eyes?*

"Is your cycle off-balance?"

My response: *Nope!*

"You know you can go to (insert country here) and adopt a child?"

My thoughts: *But there are many children here, so why go somewhere else?*

"I don't know why you're having such trouble. I got pregnant—boom! —on my first try."

My response: *Oh, really? I've heard that first-try pregnancies result in the worst kind of stretch marks and kids who eat trash.* (Ok, I didn't say that part out loud.) Wow! Good for you! (while I rolled my eyes).

And the most popular of them all …

"Drink teas."

"Stop using deodorant!"

"Are you dieting?"

"Are you having angry sex? It worked for me!"

"Does your hubby wear boxers?"

I did take some advice, like about vitamins, bone broth soup, and teas. I even tried keeping my legs up in the air for 25 minutes after the deed, even though it gave me a whopper of a headache. I was desperate! I made us try everything that seemed logical to me, like the obvious unprotected sex, rubbing a rabbit's tail, and consuming two tubs of ice cream a week. Ok, the last one was not a positive recommendation. But I did need it for my mental health.

But out of all the questions I heard, the one I asked myself over and over gnawed at me like an insatiable rodent—*Am I broken?*

So, I did what any other anxiety-ridden person (not-so wisely) would do when faced with a medical concern in the ungodly hours of the night. I turned to the internet. Majority of articles reference to, "Consult a medical professional."

We tried all the unsolicited advice—I guess it would make sense to do this.

So that was the next step.

Chapter 4

Expensive Dreams

As the endless nights dragged on, I became a Google master at finding doctors that *could not* help me. During the days I would call multiple obstetrician "OB" clinics to ask all my endless questions and hopes of getting the help to put me on the right path, and the unfortunate responses were that they either had no availability to see me, or they wouldn't take my insurance. The results of finding a fertility specialist were bleak, and under my current insurance, it was a no go. To see a fertility specialist, I would have to pay out of pocket and find someone who had availability. Who knew it was such a small market and getting an appointment was like trying to see the Pope?

After a long two weeks of researching and making calls I was able to get an appointment with a doctor who came highly recommended ... by Google, of course! Downside, he was a one-hour drive from our home. I made an appointment immediately after reviewing the website. And I was able to get one for Monday the following week.

The morning of the appointment, I was feeling surprisingly good about myself. I got dressed and did my hair and makeup. I felt more like I was going to an interview than a doctor's appointment, but my thought process was if I impressed this doctor, he would easily provide me the information I needed. Although logically that made no sense, but neither did the reasoning of why I had to see a specialist. I was so completely in the dark about my issues.

The drive there was quiet, and the scenery was incredible. The route we chose took us away from regular LA traffic.

There were mountains covered with beautiful broad trees that lined the road. The sky was a mesmerizing blue. It was a wonderful time to reflect and just let my face kiss the sun. It was the deep breaths I didn't know I needed until I made them. It's a memory somehow etched in my mind. I felt at ease.

Walking toward this clinic was like walking to a regular office building, nothing wowed me. In my mind it was just a consult, I had not really understood the severity of what I was doing. My initial mind was that it should be a quick fix. At least that was what I was hoping for.

The waiting room was quiet, low music playing and calming pastel colors on the walls that perfectly display smiling babies in some perfectly framed pictures and some taped up polaroids on the walls. I stared at them, almost mesmerized. My trans didn't really create a vision of a family. I was never the girl who thought marriage and babies were the destination of my life. So, this new act was brewing some weird feelings in me. Johnnie was quiet the entire time, and I wondered what he was feeling. My mind kept playing the scenario that this doctor would provide me a little advice and maybe some sort of vitamin or something that could fix this, and then we would walk out and boom a baby in my arms. Based on this doctor's reviews, he had worked miracles for other women. I thought surely, he could do the same for me!

As my name was called by the nurse, both Johnnie and I stood up and followed her through a doorway leading us back to a small office with light blue colored walls that held framed degrees and some accolades of Doctor Singh. A smaller man. He wore frameless glasses and held a slight smile on his face. He made eye contact with both Johnnie and me and asked a simple question in an incredibly soft voice.

"Why are you here today?"

In my mind, this is what I thought I said, "Well, after much review, you came highly recommended, as Johnnie and I are having some difficulty conceiving."

What came out of my mouth was "Uh, I um, I want a baby. And the internet said I should talk to somebody."

The doctor nodded sympathetically and even let out a chuckle (at least he spared me the "you're an idiot" look I was internally giving myself). I was a bit embarrassed, but in the big scheme of things, I had no control of my mouth. My nerves tend to take control when I am nervous.

His attentiveness and empathetic nature helped me feel at ease. In time, the quaver in my voice died away, even though my stomach continued to lurch with nervousness. He was highly informative. He began with the fancy three letters that I had Googled the crap out of—IVF—as he began explaining the different fertility options available. I was trying so hard to understand it all, but I felt like I was attending medical school and had a nice, but difficult professor in front of me. Once he began, he did not stop. I had never even heard of some of these options before, despite all my Googling. He mentioned Intrauterine Insemination (IUI) and Clomiphene Citrate (Clomid).

I had absolutely no idea what the hell he was talking about! I learned later that IUI involves washing and concentrating sperm in the uterus during ovulation, bypassing the fallopian tubes. I also learned that Clomid is an oral medication that stimulates the secretion of the follicle-stimulating hormone (FSH) and is often used to treat certain types of infertility. Wow! During the visit, he also mentioned the possibility of surrogacy, where another woman becomes pregnant through IVF using the intended parents' sperm and egg or donors. And then there was adoption, which I fully understood as I had many friends that had adopted or were adopted.

I felt overwhelmed by all the information and had to take a deep breath to hear what he was saying. *If I was in class, I would be taking notes! That's what I needed to do!* I reached for my pen and notepad, but realized I didn't have either. I frantically searched my purse, my head completely inside my bag. The doctor noticed I wasn't paying attention and passed me a small notepad and pen from his desk.

"Okay," he nodded. "Well, to know what would best work for you, we would first have some labs and an ultrasound done. We need to see what your follicle sizes look like to help us decide."

He continued, "After the results and an overall evaluation, I will be able to recommend the best course of treatment, including discussing if IVF is necessary."

Before we left, he advised me on what vitamins to take, like Vitamin C and D, Coenzyme Q10, Zinc, and Folic Acid. There was this welcomed feeling that we were approaching my situation from all angles. It was all very analytical, or as I like to say—Mandy-style! Then, we talked about the labs and imaging that I would have to do. They included:

1. Ovulation testing: This involves measuring the levels of hormones in the blood or urine to determine if/when ovulation is occurring.
2. Hysterosalpingography (HSG): This test uses an X-ray to check the shape of the uterus and fallopian tubes and to see if they are blocked or damaged.
3. Sperm analysis: This test evaluates the quantity and quality of sperm in a man's semen, which can affect fertility.
4. Laparoscopy (if needed): A surgical procedure in which they insert a small tube with a camera through a tiny incision in the abdomen to check for any pelvic or ovarian abnormalities.
5. Endometrial biopsy: This test involves taking a small sample of the lining of the uterus to check for any abnormal conditions (which he did not do).
6. Ovarian reserve testing: This test measures the quantity and quality of eggs in a woman's ovaries, which can affect fertility.

All this information was great, but I thought it was going to be much easier. I had no idea that I had opened Pandora's box. Now to find out there was an entire process we would have to go through and, on top of that, I needed to learn more fucking acronyms. My mind was in a whirlwind.

Being taken care of in this way made me feel good. I was ready. Plus, I always felt good during test-taking time in school, so I figured this would be a breeze.

Well, I was wrong. As I would find out within the next couple of weeks, my school tests had nothing on the kinds of tests I had to take for this process. It was extremely un-fun (to put it mildly). But I mean we wanted a baby! So, I pushed forward.

A few days later we received a call from Dr. Singh's office to come in and discuss our lab results. Another one-hour drive before I would learn my fate, which was a bit nerve-racking—to say the least. I had no idea what to expect again. *Did I pass or fail? Was this a yes or no type of conversation? Or was it a Jerry Springer type of move, "You are not the mother" scenario?*

Once we got back to the doctor's office and were seated again across the same small desk, we quickly learned that Johnnie had robust sperm (yay!)— The doctor put it gently that his sperm were plentiful, they had a bit of a directional issue, where they would swim in opposite directions and not in a formation group. Basically, they went wherever they pleased. Johnnie was very proud of his high-quality sperm and plentiful guys, even jumping up from his chair in excitement (to my horror).

Apparently, his sperm mimicked his genetic background. And he knew it. "Aye, my swimmers are always ready to make that Irish exit," Johnnie joked.

The doctor didn't know how to respond to that (I mean, how do you really respond to something like that?), so he simply smiled and shifted his focus to me and my labs.

He informed me that at 37 years old, my eggs were as healthy and abundant as a 25-year-old woman's eggs. *Yay! Suck it, young girls!* He also said my FSH levels were normal, and my other labs came back normal.

I did mention to him I was told I had endometriosis. He said that should not cause any issues. (Later, as I began to educate myself on my body, I found out that he was wrong.)

So… what was going on? Did my eggs not like a good St. Paddy's Day parade or something? I mean, it's the day we met. Or were his Irish exits exiting my eggs' invitations?

Our first reaction to this news was, of course, relief and happiness. He had sperm. I had eggs. That means baby! Google knew that, even I did! But that reaction soon turned to confusion. What was the issue, then?

Was it the result of too many club nights?

Endless happy hours?

Was it from having mammograms?

Deodorants?

A meat-based diet?

Regular manicures?

What?

Why were two successful, mature, happy, and committed adults who both decided—and desired—to have a child, struggling?

Admittedly, I was spiraling.

The doctor tried to ease my confusion by offering his suggestion to approach this with IVF. Although I felt confident in my knowledge of In Vitro Fertilization (I finally had those damn letters down) at this point, I was still unsure about doing it. He momentarily walked out of the office, leaving me confused about why, then came back in with a young woman with brunette colored hair and wearing blue scrubs.

"This is Lisa. She is our coordinator. She will provide you with what happens next," he said.

She said hello and then Dr. Singh exited the office. We tried to make some pleasant small talk, but we were so confused. I remember looking over at Johnnie wondering if he was as confused as I was, or if he was still in a place of utter bliss about his superpowered sperm (even if they were drunk!). My mind was racing. *Why did he leave? Were we doing more tests? Did we decide on the next course of action, and I don't remember? He made a recommendation, but that was it.*

Lisa began her intro with what the next steps will entail and that she was there to assist us with the costs and scheduling of the process. Feeling very confused as to just what had happened, we both just sat there to hear what she had to say.

"Okay, so before we go any further, do you smoke?"

I responded, "No," and Johnnie shook his head no as well.

"Any recreational drugs?"

We both spoke out "No" at the same time.

"What about alcohol?"

I responded "Ahh Yes!

"What type of alcohol?"

"Wine," I responded with a smile and looked over at Johnnie.

"How much do you consume? And how often?"

I responded with, "A bottle."

And she instantly responded back with, "A BOTTLE??"

At this point, she began to make me nervous. So, I said, "He drinks a bottle, I only do a glass?"

I could feel Johnnie looking at me in shock. I quickly glanced over at him and shrugged my shoulders. I wasn't going to be judged harshly and I didn't have it in me to say the weekend before we had multiple bottles, and I was totally drunk. Her disapproving expression made me throw Johnnie under the bus.

While I sat their fidgeting listening to her intently. She then went on about costs for the procedure as insurance didn't cover any of it. I had absolutely no idea about the costs of having a baby, even in a 'typical' situation. But being the planner I am, I felt confident about my calculations. *Five thousand dollars should cover it*, I confidently said to myself. It was a lot of money, but I knew Johnnie and I could manage that. I smiled at the young woman as she caught my eye and gave her a nod. *Let's see how close I am!*

She smiled back. And after letting her fingers fly over her keyboard for a few minutes, she announced.

"So, treatments per session will typically total about $50,000 …"

I stopped hearing anything else at that point. I swear I felt like my soul almost left my body in hearing those numbers.

"Fifty thousand dollars? Holy shit!" I blurted out loud.

Johnnie looked at me and started laughing at my outburst. These types of outbursts usually seem very entertaining to him. And, as usual, he chimed in with a joke, "Do you accept monopoly money?"

Lisa smiled as if she had heard that one before. But my 'holy shit' outburst made her more curious at me. Seriously, though, I thought—*With that amount, the doctor could pay for a small plane.*

"We would collect half of the total today," she continued, not missing a beat.

When I found my voice, I croaked, *"Half? NOW?"*

She nodded back at me, "Yes."

I responded with "Ahh, the doctor mentioned that sometimes, it could take up to three tries of IVF, so is that all part of the amount you just mentioned?"

"No," she replied.

"And there's no guarantee that the treatments will work?" I came back with a rebuttal question, as my mind continued to process this added information.

Lisa shook her head robotically. She had clearly been through these questions before.

"Unfortunately, that would be up to you and the doctor and how many sessions you do. But there is no guarantee, and we don't like to promise anything."

I remember looking over at Johnnie in total astonishment, like, *Dude, WTF!* *(head node)* We silently spoke to each other with our eyes.

Is she fucking crazy? And he looked back at me with, *Dude, WTF! She had to be crazy. Plus, we don't have that kind of money!*

I could always count on him to hear me without hearing me.

We both smiled politely at the coordinator and asked for some documents to review at home. We stood up quickly, not wanting to show her how anxious we were to leave the office. We didn't even let her go over all the payment options. I mean, seriously, what was the fucking point? There weren't any workable options for $50,000. We didn't have that kind of money and saying that number out loud made me feel like I had to poop! (My fight-or-flight responses are a bit jacked up. My recourse for fear is to poop—I don't know why, but it is.)

In my mind, when I thought about $50,000 (not that I thought about it much) to help me understand what I was getting into would be a scenario something like this: We would walk into a fancy car dealership. The salesperson sells me their top-of-the-line vehicle for a whopping $50,000. He says it was the best on the market, but there was a catch. I had to pay for it in full (and non-refundable) before driving it off the lot. "And oh, by the way, we cannot guarantee that the car will work." Once I left the dealership, I couldn't return it. Buying this car was a complete roll of the dice.

Well, WTF!!!!

Our drive home from the clinic was filled with silence, defeat, and panic. Neither of us knew how to process this price tag or what to do next. Even if we somehow came up with the money, it would leave us broke or, at a minimum, extremely in debt. We wouldn't even be able to afford to raise a child *if* the treatments were successful! And it was a big *if*. Irony at its finest there.

"We can't do it," I said out loud to Johnnie.

Feeling the weight of my words crushing me where I sat on in the passenger seat, I continued (I think more for myself than Johnnie), "Let's just take it off the table."

I turned my head to look out the window, a tear rolling down my face, not wanting Johnnie to see the defeat and anguish I knew was clearly visible, especially to him. I stared out the window the entire drive home. Feeling broken and beat down. Making this decision made sense financially, but damn, it hurt like hell. Knowing the opportunity to build a family was right there, and we couldn't do it.

My mind began to play all possible options and it came right back to the original plan. We know that he had good sperm (drunk or not), and I had eggs that were fruitful and healthy for now. It wasn't over. We would have to keep trying to get pregnant the old-fashioned way.

And that was the plan to go ahead and do it that way.

Chapter 5

Bargain Shopping

For months we went ahead and did it the old fashion way, but pregnancy test after pregnancy test came back negative. It began to take a toll on my mind and spirit.

I found myself reimagining our options over-and-over again and it felt like this was simply our fate. Having a baby wasn't in the cards for us. I tried to just be 'normal' and go day-by-day, but I found myself doing absolutely nothing on the weekends, which wasn't like me at all. Plus, for the previous months, I had spent hours upon hours on the weekends researching and educating myself about fertility treatments, doctors, and IVF. Although the doctor we saw gave us other options, it seemed like the cost of it all made it nothing more than a fairy tale—a nice story to imagine, but completely out of reach.

One day, while I waited in line at my local grocery store, I noticed the pregnant woman in front of me. *Of course, I did!* Every single day after that last appointment, all I ever saw were pregnant women everywhere, just like before. But recently, the awkwardness and sadness I felt before were gone. Now it was envy and anger that surged through my body. I was pissed when I saw them. There was so much emotion watching babies, moms, strollers, and baby commercials. It enveloped me. I would try to remind myself that it wasn't their fault, and it wasn't my fault either, which was much harder than expected. I was diligently trying to find a way to heal and be okay with our circumstances.

But this time at the grocery store was different. I thought I was finally okay with not having a baby. I didn't feel mad or sad. This lady had a glow about her I had never noticed before in other women. I watched her hands gently cradling her stomach. She protectively placed her hand over her belly while waiting for her turn to push the cart.

I couldn't bring myself to feel any negativity toward her. I rarely go around complimenting people, especially pregnant women, but this time I felt the urge to say something.

"You look so beautiful," I said, smiling at her, expecting nothing in return.

"Thank you so much," she said, her cheeks flushing with pride. "I had to do fertility treatments, and I'm so happy it worked."

My heart leaped into my throat. *What did she just say? Why did she say that to me?* And immediately my mind thought she must have a lot of money. I kept my smile and put my head down not wanting her to see the questions whirling through my head. As she kept her eyes on me, I looked up at her and said, "Really? I've been thinking about looking into treatment myself. I'm just not sure we can afford it."

She enthusiastically told me about her experience, how great her doctor was, and how much he helped her through the process.

"He's amazing, seriously, and he's not that far from here. He's good at what he does, and best of all, his costs are cheaper than other doctors" she said.

It was like an invisible barrier evaporated between us.

Cheaper? Hmm, wait a minute! So, do doctors have different prices? I had not even thought of bargain shopping for a baby! My mom is a bargain shopper, and she raised me to be a great bargain shopper. Why didn't we think of looking around for someone cheaper?

I believe things happen for a reason. Like, when I first heard about IVF over lunch that day, it got me to understand something I hadn't before—I had the F struggles. Now that I was hearing about this F word again from another pregnant stranger with the added cost reduction, it felt somehow like a sign. Were we meant to cross paths that fateful day? Was my trip to the grocery store about more than stocking the refrigerator or stocking my womb?

By the end of our conversation, my opinion on my path to this life with a child had changed. I needed to get my shit together and get back on track! I wrote the name of the doctor and the clinic down on my notepad (I had it this time) and enthusiastically thanked her. I never thought to ask for her name or number, and she didn't ask for mine. And despite my returning to that store many times afterward, I never saw her again.

As I strolled my cart to my car with more energy, faith, and hope than I had had in months. I felt something stir inside that I hadn't felt in a very long time. I got into my car and my mind was racing with how to tell Johnnie, how to really sell it to him. Or maybe I had to sell it to myself? I was the one who really made the final decision. So, now I've changed my mind! *What the hell is going on with me?*

I rushed home and googled the crap out of this doctor that lovely pregnant woman shared with me. Mr. Google, along with multiple reviews, said that this doctor was a miracle worker. And he really was cheaper. Cheaper sounds like a dirty word in the fertility world (or in any medical setting), but in our world, it sounded only like one thing—POSSIBILITY! Wow, this doctor had me wrapped around his fingers just via my computer screen. All I had to do was read the countless testimonials—And I was sold!

This doctor must be a superhero if he is offering such a fantastical plan. *Can you imagine if there was a pay-for-play strategy? You only pay if you're successful, and that child can start chipping in for the cost at 18.* I know, I know, it sounds like a ridiculous payment program in this capitalist market we live in. Still, the thoughts and feelings were released like floodgates.

I worked my magic and got Johnnie to agree to give it another go. Honestly, it didn't take much convincing. He was onboard with the word 'cheaper.' I think he was also tired of me scheduling our sexy time. And he was relieved to see some light back in my eyes.

I was full of excitement and, once again in a tap of a keyboard, I booked a consultation appointment. But this time, it was with a doctor I believed could help us because of the element of costs.

I convinced myself that this doctor, Doctor Smilken, was the best of the best. The night before the appointment, I read multiple raving reviews from his patients for the hundredth time. I prepped a very casual but confident outfit. I ironed it and laid out my jewelry to match. The stars, I was sure, were aligning. I had not one, but *two*, chance encounters with women who told me about their successes. These weren't coincidences. *I didn't believe in those anyway. This was a higher power pointing me in the direction I kept missing.*

That morning, I felt good. My outfit was looking good, makeup was on point, my hair had seen better days, but was still looking good. I felt good. Johnnie and I matched in colors, not intentionally, but it was super cute. I grabbed a bigger handbag, loaded my notes and labs from previous doctor, and was ready. Both Johnnie and I walked into the fertility clinic with our heads held high and a medical file stuffed with glowing reports about the state of our drunk sperm and youthful eggs tucked under my arm.

What could possibly go wrong?

Chapter 6

Resignation to the Fertility God

I tapped my foot with nervous excitement as I looked around the waiting area. While sterile in the usual "doctor's office" kind of way, cheerful framed pictures of pregnant women hanging on the walls with their faces beaming as their hands caressed their big bellies, warmed it up. (Okay, the posters once again screamed "stock photos" rather than "satisfied patients," but they were still effective.) I couldn't help picturing myself again among them, hair flowing, skin glowing, smiling brightly at the perfectly symmetrical belly that was blossoming under my sundress…

I'm going to be on that wall, I thought to myself. I could see it! But when I swept an admiring glance over the pictures for a second time, I noticed something else—there wasn't one single photo of a woman of color. I then took a quick scan of the room itself (making polite eye contact with some of the other women who also sat waiting) and noticed that there weren't any other women of color in the office *in real life*, either.

While this gave me pause, I didn't want my spirits dampened before seeing the doctor. *No! I was just so excited! I am not letting anything change that.* So, I pumped myself up by pushing away my concerns. *It's time to meet this miracle maker! Let's go!*

We finally made our way to the infamous Dr. Smilken, it was time for our consultation. They collected $250.00 in advance for this. So, it better make a world of a difference. A nurse finally called my name, and I looked over at Johnnie. He nodded, took my hand, and we got up together.

The nurse led us through a narrow hallway, then down another corridor, and into the last office in the back. I never noticed that many doctors' offices have this narrow walkway—*Was it planned that way?* I noticed my mind wandering to the most insignificant things, that I had to bring my thoughts back to here and now.

As we entered the room, the doctor didn't look up to greet us—no eye contact whatsoever. He immersed himself in the enormous stack of papers set on top of his battered oak desk. He just gestured toward the chairs and asked us our names and how we felt.

"Hello, my name is Mandy, and this is Johnnie. We are doing especially well since you came so highly recommended." And that is exactly how it came out of my mouth this time.

I figured he would look up at that and say, "Yes, I am here to make your dreams come true."

But he still didn't look up and continued to read a file that was not mine. *Okay, I'm trying to keep my temper under control, but seriously, WTF?*

For a moment, I worried we had the wrong doctor. *This couldn't be him!* I gazed around the room for some clue to say I was in the wrong place, but I knew I wasn't because he looked just like the photo, I had seen on the website. An older white man (like most fertility experts I found) in his mid-sixties. He had chubby cheeks, no real neck to be seen, and eyes that squinted behind wire-rimmed glasses. But I didn't want to judge a book by its cover. The quiet man across from us may not have been impressive to look at, but he was the man who would make our dreams come true—even if, as it appeared, he had no manners.

When he finally looked up and said, "Hmmm ok, Mandy and Johnnie?"

It was as if he didn't hear me make the introduction a few seconds ago. Still, I immediately perked up at the sound of my own name.

"These are for you," I told the doctor, handing over the documentation, my excitement causing me to tremble visibly. Johnnie reached out and gave my hand a squeeze. I could feel my pulse beating in my palm.

Still (oddly) not meeting my eyes, the doctor opened the file and read. Then, stopping almost immediately, he cleared his throat and said, "So … you're 37 years old?"

"Yes. Well, I will be 38 next month."

"Then, I'll first need you to remember that you're old."

My temper was starting to bubble. *Seriously, WTF?*

I could feel my expression of hopeful excitement slide off my face. "That's not ... old...." I giggled slightly and glanced at Johnnie, subconsciously reaching over, and putting my hand on the file to draw his attention to all the other papers he had yet to read. There were all our test results still to consider. *I had great eggs!*

"It *is* old."

What the hell? I laughed incredulously. *Aren't most women who visit this clinic over 30 years old?* My story wasn't exactly unique.

"Um, I know I am a little older than the recommended age for starting a family, but the doctor I saw before said my eggs looked healthy and ..."

The doctor cut me off with a sigh and waved his hand. *"Look,"* he said, finally meeting my eyes, "I'm asking you to recognize your age."

My stomach churned with rage as my eyes darted between him, Johnnie, and the medical file.

"Yes, I am aware of my age." I raised my voice to give him a fuller taste of some New York snark.

"Every year, I celebrate my birthday, and I know how to count."

This mutha fucking doctor didn't seem to understand the sarcasm and just looked at me. *Did he think I was an idiot?*

"If we are to continue down this path. You need to understand that you are old, and because of your age, there is a high possibility this won't work" he said.

This was it. I lost it. I began to burn and boil inside. There was no stopping this. I leaned over to Johnnie and said (not in a whisper), "If this fucking guy says I'm old one more time, I swear I'm going to leap over this mutha fucking desk and stab him in the eye with his own pencil."

Rage just flowed over me. I couldn't hold any emotion back. I could feel my heart racing and the blood spiraling through my veins. I began shaking with the effort of holding back my tears.

I was screaming on the inside—*Why won't you look me in the eye? Why won't you want to read the rest of my labs? Why are you so hung up on me saying I am old? Why do you want to ruin this for me? Why? Why?*

Johnnie grabbed my hand to steady me. He knew I had expected a lot from this appointment and noticed my crushed state.

"I believe we've established her age," Johnnie told the doctor firmly.

"Now, I think it would be in the best interest for the both of us if we just moved on."

Neither the doctor nor I could move on. *Who does this old-ass fuck think he is, telling me I'm old? How fucking dare, he?*

The rest of the appointment—which lasted all of fifteen minutes, tops— seemed to crawl by. I don't even know what else he even talked about. It had been over for me. When I first stepped into that office, I felt so good. So confident. Now I felt the rug ripped right out from under me. I had made the mistake of making this doctor up to be an emphatic fertility god without even meeting him.

We left the office, but with each step, it felt like my feet were filled with cement. The emotions were so strong they consumed me, that I just followed Johnnie's lead. A nurse called out to us and asked if we wanted to have a discussion with the financial department, and I turned to her and screamed "NO," as we continued to walk out. Screw the 'cheaper.' Now I knew why he was cheaper—it was because he could be an asshole for the sticker price.

Now, another silent car ride home. But there wasn't much silence in my head. I was stuck in a loop. That was our best chance. And now I possibly threw it away because of my emotions?

Was it all a hustle to take my hard-earned $250.00 for a 15-minute visit? What was his problem? Did my emotions ruin this possibility?

"We can still try with this doctor," Johnnie said. breaking the icy silence with false cheer. "I mean, we shouldn't give up just because he used the 'O' word?"

I stared out the window. No tears this time. I was too angry.

"I doubt he'll be doing most of the treatments anyway," Johnnie continued.

I shot him a deadly glare but said nothing. Meanwhile, my mind was raging. *Are you crazy? I'm never going back to him or to any other asshole doctor who insists on telling me I'm old!*

I knew I wasn't as young as most women who got pregnant in the blink of an eye. But I was only 37. I knew of women in their 40s who had babies. Those women had experienced all the sleepless nights, mounds of dirty diapers, and vomit-stained T-shirts.

"Babe, are you okay?"

When Johnnie broke the silence with his sweet question, it made me want to leap out of my skin and just attack. *Of course, I wasn't okay! Wasn't it obvious?* But I remained silent, sitting with my arms crossed and frowning so hard it was like I had permanently sculpted the expression onto my face.

When we finally pulled into our driveway, Johnnie parked the car. Gripping the steering wheel, he looked over at me and tried again.

"You know, babe, some doctors don't always have the best bedside manners. It doesn't mean he's not a good doctor or that the treatment won't work. So even if he didn't leave the best first impression," he said.

"NO!" I responded loudly. "I want someone who has a better bedside manner than that!"

And suddenly, I was going through a list Johnnie hadn't asked for.

"I want someone who looks me in the eye! I want someone who has faith that this will happen to me or at least believes in the science that says this can work! Someone who sees me as a person with feelings and emotions. That is what I want. I want someone to tell me this will happen and that we will have a baby!"

As soon as I finished stating my demands, I burst into tears. And then more tears. I sat there in the car and cried my eyes out. At that moment, I only wanted to be alone with my grief. To recoil into my misery and disappear for a bit. But Johnnie wouldn't give up.

"We'll keep looking then. We will find someone else who has the right bedside manner. Plus, all those other things."

"We? We?" I exploded, all while crying. "I'm the one who's done all the research and work by myself! There's no 'we' here. This has all been on me, and it's all gone to shit!"

I knew in my heart that Johnnie meant well, but at that point, I was beyond reasoning. He parked the car and I stormed into the house to stew in my own juices for a while. My wounds prevented me from being around him. All I kept doing was asking myself over and over in my head what I had done to deserve my childless fate. Thoughts raced through my head—*Why did I wait so long to want to have a baby? Why was I so ignorant to the fact that we weren't getting pregnant sooner? Would it have changed things if we started this all sooner? At least then, he couldn't call me old! And did I lose control with Dr. Asshole? Did I fuck this up on purpose? Was I sure I wanted a baby? Was I unreasonable? What was happening to me?*

Meanwhile, Johnnie was a gentleman—literally, a gentle man. He left me alone and spent the day in the kitchen. I knew this because I could hear pots and pans clanging against one another while some music played lightly somewhere in the background. After a while, the aroma of my favorite dish began wafting into the room.

While I was miserable enough to stay in my room and go without eating for the rest of the evening, the thought of how I'd lashed out at Johnnie haunted me. I had to apologize to him. He had been nothing but supportive and by my side this whole time. He didn't deserve my outlash.

My first step out of bed toward the door felt so overwhelming. I just wanted to crumble into pieces, but I pushed forward. When I met him in the kitchen, he'd already set the table for both of us. And when he caught sight of me, he pulled out my chair, kissed the top of my head, and began serving the amazing dinner he'd prepared for me.

I managed a small smile, "Thanks for backing me up with that doctor."

"Of course. I support you—no matter what."

"Yeah?" I asked, my voice cracking. "Would you still support me if I gave up?"

Something had changed in me over the past five hours. I was done with this baby business—for real this time. Johnnie and I had been happy before we'd gotten involved with this. We had traveled, had wonderful careers, enjoyed our friends and family and good health. Why had I felt a need to change all of that? Why couldn't things stay the same? The two of us had to be enough to be a family.

"Babe," Johnnie said, "I'm not ready to give up yet. But I'll allow you the space to think things over."

"I'll think about it," I said to him.

I didn't end the day researching infertility online like before. Instead, we just went to bed. As Johnnie drifted off to sleep, I couldn't stop thinking about our journey so far. I knew that the reason I embarked on this relentless quest was not only to find the best fertility doctor, medical expertise, or high success rates. It was about the recent desire to become a parent.

There were issues with location, finances, harsh judgments, drunk sperm, being looked at as a statistic instead of a person, and the complete lack of a bedside manner (and eye contact). The combination of it all made me feel like motherhood was slipping away, and that emotional pain was unbearable.

However, the most profound blow to my emotions came from the repeated reminding of my age, reinforcing the anxiety that time was running out. For the first time I could hear the clock ticking louder with each passing day.

As the night progressed, it turned blue in the moonlight, and finally, as it slowly brightened into a warm, orangey glow with the rising of the sun.

I didn't sleep at all that night.

Chapter 7

Botanical Beauty & Uninvited Guests

Most of my adult life, I had a very subdued version of OCD—my "just right" obsessive-compulsive disorder. But after that last doctor's appointment, my mental and emotional health took a nosedive and my OCD skyrocketed. Even though I genuinely believed that I was *not* old, the daily struggle to beat his words away from my head became exhausting.

I worked to keep my mind preoccupied with anything and everything else. Luckily, I had just the thing to lift me out of my funk ... my upcoming wedding.

A few months earlier, Johnnie and I had flown to New York for Christmas and had stayed at a friend's apartment while she was away. Unfortunately, my period, along with my endometriosis that I had known about for years, but not known about its impact on my fertility, showed its face and came in with a vengeance, terrorizing my body. I spent most of our visit curled up in a ball, popping Tylenol, and hugging hot pads to my body. I was miserable and in excruciating pain.

By the time New Year's Eve rolled around, I was still in pain and expecting to spend the day as I had all the others—watching TV, wrapped in a blanket, and sipping hot tea. But Johnnie clearly felt otherwise. He began hassling me.

"Come on, let's go out! It's New Year's Eve!"

I gave him a look like, you're kidding, right? *Wasn't it obvious by my low energy that I wasn't going anywhere? Didn't he see the dark circles that had been tattooed under my eyes all week?*

But he kept insisting. "You will feel better after you take a shower. And we can find someplace warm..." *Blah blah blah.* That's all I heard.

Finally, I agreed to go, although more out of guilt than anything else. I felt bad about how my cramps had put a cramp on everything else over the holidays. If I didn't go out with him now, our entire holiday season would end up being a bust because of me.

Since we were already staying in Brooklyn, he had decided we should go check out the Brooklyn Botanical Garden. As I layered myself up to enter the treacherous winter New York was having that year, I played out options of how I could convince Johnnie to head back home sooner rather than later. We weren't in the cab for five minutes when I began regretting my decision to go. I wasn't feeling it. I mean, who goes to the Botanical Gardens in the winter, anyway? The only thing I was feeling was the abdominal pain that refused to give me any relief whatsoever.

It was cold and dark when we arrived. Johnnie, being incredibly determined, led me to a conservatory that was indoors and climate controlled, so it was nice and warm. Plus, the pavilion was lit in such a way that it was like being outdoors on a sunny day. Seeing all the flowers and plants in bloom lifted my spirits a little. I didn't want to admit to him there that the space itself gave me some joy. Just walking in the environment did something to my soul. But the pain was still there, I couldn't deny it. I was ready to go. The little bit of energy I had was depleted and my face and body said we were done. Unfortunately, Johnnie wasn't. He had this great idea of wanting to take a photo of me amongst all the vibrant colors.

Oh my God! Why? I thought to myself, groaning aloud. I was not feeling pretty or smiley and was not at all up for pictures.

"Let's get a photo," Johnnie said.

I forced a smile. When he looked it over, he said, "I think we need to take another one."

He showed it to me. It was as horrible … as I knew it would be. It needed to be retaken. He politely asked if I could retake it. As annoyed as I was, I told myself, try to give him a genuine smile. The sooner he takes a decent picture, the sooner we will get to go home.

I turned to him with a sigh. "Okay. Let's take another."

I closed my eyes and then I slowly opened them, prepped with a smile that should have been better than the last one. And just as I opened my eyes, Johnnie dropped to one knee and held up a ring.

I gasped, "What are you doing?"

"What does it look like I'm doing?" Johnnie asked. "Will you marry me?"

"No!" I blurted. Shaking uncontrollably.

I could see Johnnie nearly fall over. "No?"

In my defense, I hadn't meant "No." It had slipped out because I had been thinking, "No way. Is this really happening right now?"

Luckily, Johnnie figured it was something like that because he said, "I'm going to ask you one more time ..."

And I said it again. "No! Not no! I mean, yes! Yes! I just wasn't ready for this."

In retrospect, if I was him, I would have gotten up and walked away with that ring if I had asked someone to marry me, and they blurted out NO. *Twice!* But this sweet, patient man knew my body had taken over my brain, and he knew how much I wanted to marry him.

Relieved, Johnnie slipped the ring on my finger, and I suddenly felt a lot better. *What cramps?* My body must have been flooded with oxytocin or some other happiness hormone after the proposal because I was no longer in pain. And I was more than ready to pose for more pictures—this time with a genuine smile on my face.

Six months later, we were planning a wedding, and it helped bring a smile back to my face. Instead of making the daily dive into infertility blogs, I was now spending my time researching wedding venues.

And rather than trying to figure out the best doctor in our area, I was looking for the best baker to make our wedding cake. It gave me something happy to focus on and celebrate. Celebrating my love for Johnnie was something far better to focus on.

We knew it would be in New York. A few months later, we flew back to start the planning. A dear friend referred us to a wedding planner named Jacqueline of "Lifetime Events" to help us from Los Angeles. She was incredibly detailed-oriented and a tremendous help in organizing all my scattered ideas. This amazing woman kept me on track during a time when I was juggling every emotion possible ensuring that our wedding day would be truly memorable. *Our checklist was looking good. Venue-Check. A date-Check. DJ hired-Check, Said "Yes" to the dress-Check, Cake and so on.* Everything was going as planned until one day, as we were reviewing tablecloths and napkins, Jaqueline asked us about including children at the wedding. Her question was about incorporating them into the desserts and festivities, but to me, the question meant me seeing happy children, babies and happy parents.

I immediately felt sadness and without hesitation, I quickly responded, "No!"

I could see the shock and curiosity in her eyes, but she didn't press further and moved on with our to-do list. I glanced at Johnnie, wondering if my abrupt reaction made me seem cold and mean. I began wondering if it were even possible to say no to guests and if so, how could we get away with making such a request without exposing that excruciating pain to everyone else?

Both Johnnie and I went back and forth about the thought of not seeing family or friends because of my decision. My mind played scenarios after scenarios of each interaction and each one came back with me not feeling good about myself.

I needed an out without sharing all of what we have been through. What we came up with was lying that the venue would charge us per head, and we had limited headcount.

It broke my heart to lie to so many people, but I felt it was the only way. When we finally made that decision, I sighed with a deep sense of relief.

On Thursday, October 3rd was our wedding day. The ceremony was held on the deck overlooking the Long Island Sound. It was a lovely day when Johnnie and I exchanged vows. Everything went smoothly ... until the reception.

As we basked in the joy of our nuptials, a couple approached us to offer their good wishes in hand with a baby. I noticed the little bundle cradled in the woman's arms, and I couldn't mask my shock. The mother noticed my surprise, and, with a sly smile, she cooed, "Don't worry. This little one won't cost you a dime for dinner. I've got nature's pantry right here." And with a suggestive wink, she pulled her baby even closer to her chest.

A wave of sadness washed over me, but I couldn't let it show, not on my wedding day. Instead, I forced a smile, and after a quick exchange of pleasantries, I made our exit clear, "Well, okay! We need to go say hi to some guests." I pulled Johnnie along with me, walking away from the perfect picture of motherhood.

Once we were out of earshot, I turned on Johnnie. "Didn't I say I did not want any children here?"

They were his friends. *Why didn't he know they were going to bring their baby?* I was fuming.

Johnnie protested. "I didn't say they could bring their baby! Don't forget, babe, people don't know what we are going through."

I felt myself deflating. He was right, of course. But the sight of the baby had unsettled me. Until that moment, I had been so good at pushing away the emptiness I was feeling.

"Come on," Johnnie said. "Let's dance."

Yet, of all the things that happened on our wedding day, the ones I remember most were the two baby wedding crasher ... and ending up in the hospital.

Chapter 8

Seizing Clarity

A friend of ours had agreed to drive our car back to the hotel after the wedding. He must have had a fun time because he was a bit tipsy when it was time to leave. As both Johnnie and I watched his demeanor, we decided it would not be a good idea to get in the car with him or even let him drive. So, instead, we joined our friends and family on the bus we had rented for our guests. We weren't done celebrating anyway, and so we would take the party back with us to the hotel where we were all staying.

We crowded together, laughing at the scene I created as I gathered my dress around me and settled into the tight but comfy, padded seats. The laughter and chatter didn't let up as we got on the road and bounced along the freeway. Suddenly, I felt very dizzy and noticed that the headlights of passing cars seemed to flash by creating double vision. I tried shaking the feeling, but it started to get much more intense.

What is going on with me? I wondered.

Then the bus lurched forward, the world around me swayed, and I broke into a sweat that began seeping through the bodice of my wedding dress.

What is happening?

My heart raced, and my breaths came short and fast. I gasped!

"I need air… I need air…."

"What?" People around me began jumping to attention.

"I can't breathe…"

Since I was wearing a very fitted, hourglass-style dress, Johnnie assumed I was sitting in a way that cut off my air.

"It's the dress! It's the dress! Unzip her. Give her air!" someone yelled.

Johnnie unzipped me, but the relief it provided was minimal. My head felt like it was about to detach from my body and float away at any minute.

I panicked, screaming, "I need to get off this bus! Now!"

I heard screaming at the driver to stop the bus, saying that I was sick. Around me, I could hear people debating whether I was just drunk. I could hear Johnnie say, "She's only had soda and water tonight."

"I need to get off this bus! Now! Pull over! Pull over!"

"I can't pull over here!" the driver said back. "But don't worry. We're getting off this next exit. Just hang on!"

It felt like I was holding myself together for an eternity, but it was just minutes later, the driver was able to pull over right in front of the hotel.

I wanted to bolt off the bus, but I was still feeling too fuzzy to move that fast. So instead, I got up from my seat holding out my hands to keep my balance. The effort felt like climbing Everest.

Once I stepped outside, a light breeze offered me a few seconds of relief before my eyes rolled into the back of my head and I *felt* myself falling backward. Somehow, I was now looking down at myself on the cold concrete. I was outside and above my body. And then I drifted. I was in some sort of empty space; it seemed familiar but not something I couldn't put my finger on. I looked around and then I saw this small floating silhouette of a child approaching me. I squinted a bit to see.

It was a little girl.

Her light brown curls framed her face beautifully and her brown eyes twinkled as she smiled at me. She stood there in front of me, playing and dancing around, looking at me every now and then to give me her comforting smile. All I could see past her was a moving silhouette of people but could not recognize them.

When I finally was able to focus and see clearly, I woke up in the emergency room hooked up to an IV. My wedding dress off and my hair freed from the beautiful updo. As I slowly opened my eyes, I saw that Johnnie was holding my hand.

"You passed out once we walked off the bus," Johnnie explained, a worried look in his eyes.

"I feel like I remember that" I responded.

"I had to grab your head before you hit the concrete. You scared the shit out of me," he said.

I didn't have it in me to say anything else. I was so confused about where I was and why I was there. How could this happen to me on my wedding day?

I could hear the ER doctor telling Johnnie that there was a possibility I may have been drunk and that they see this all the time. Johnnie argued with him that he knew when I was and wasn't drunk. He knew that because he knew me. He told him that I had made the decision not to drink on our wedding day.

After some tests and blood work, they saw that there was no alcohol in my system. And they had no idea what happened. The doctor suggested I see a specialist because all he could conclude was there was a possibility that I had a seizure.

We were back in Los Angeles a few weeks later and I had a tough time remembering a lot of our wedding day. I couldn't even recall our vows, even while looking longingly at the pictures of us saying them. It hurt my heart that I lost memories of the most wonderful day I had ever had.

I scheduled a doctor's appointment to see what had happened. I had undergone various tests, and the weight of uncertainty and fear weighed heavily on my mind. The thought of not knowing what was happening to my body was incredibly frightening. Finally, the results came back that I had a seizure triggered by the flashing lights of passing cars, and the swaying of the bus, called motion-sensitive seizures.

I couldn't stop thinking about what had happened when I was lying on the concrete. Although I couldn't remember much of our wedding day, I could very vividly remember the little girl I saw, who I knew instinctively was the same little girl I saw when I had gotten into a car accident years before.

Why did this sweet child's face surface in my mind every time I lost consciousness? Who was she? Was she me? Or someone else?

Chapter 9

Persuasion Abroad

"Now that you've tied the knot... when do you plan on starting a family?"

Isn't that what everybody asks from the minute after you've said your "I dos?" My parents were no exception, despite them knowing the troubles we had had in the past.

My parents are both from Trinidad. They both go back and forth to their homeland often. On one of their trips, my dad heard an ad on the radio about a clinic in Trinidad and immediately called me. He has always been the type of person that wants to help, so this was clearly in his nature to do this without understanding the situation.

"I heard on the radio about a fertility clinic here in Trinidad. I think you should check it out," he said adamantly.

"Thanks, Dad," I said. "But we can't afford it. It's too expensive."

"Oh, but if you do it here, I can be here for you and whatever you need. You and Johnnie can come here and make this a little vacation. You won't have to worry about anything," my dad said.

He went on and on about Trinidad, maybe the therapy we need and away from the big city could be helpful.

"Okay, Okay," I agreed, more to make him happy than anything else, "I'll look into it."

What I really thought when I hung up the phone was, *Hell, no! I'm not going to another country to do this! That sounds like a horrible idea.* I'd heard horror stories of bad things happening abroad. It all seemed too risky. Anyway, how could anywhere else have better treatment than the U.S.? I was naïve enough to assume that we had the most advanced medical treatments available worldwide—isn't that what we're meant to believe?

For about two months, my dad would call or text repeatedly to see if I had "looked into" the clinic he mentioned. My appeasing response was, "I am a little busy, but I'll look into it. I promise!" After a while, I was sure he was tired of me making the same empty promises repeatedly. Luckily, he is as stubborn as I am, and he didn't let up. And because of that pestering, I finally did what I said I would do—*I looked into it.*

Hello again, Google!

The clinic in Trinidad turned out to be a sister clinic to another one in Barbados, which had a lot more articles on it and reviews. I gasped when I saw that its success rate was higher than the rates I'd seen for clinics here. I was shocked. *You mean, the U.S. was not the best of the best after all? Could that be right?*

Just a few days before, Johnnie and I had dinner with some friends. It was one of those fun social gatherings where everyone is comfortable enough to pour their hearts out, while still having fun, and then we got to talking about the wild world of fertility treatments. One of the couples told us about this clinic they had tried that was like the fertility equivalent of a bulk store, with ten women in a room, all handed the same medication as if they are in a giant pharmaceutical candy store. And if it worked for you, great! You got lucky and walked away spending a cool twenty-eight grand, like you just snagged a bargain on Black Friday. But here is the kicker—for the others, they had to try something else, and the bill just kept piling up. They were telling their patients, "Hey, be ready to shell out around one hundred and twelve grand, give or take, and we'll see if you get a baby out of the deal."

I mean, talk about sticker shock, right? It felted like some of these doctors had a secret mantra: "Make money off the couples who want to have babies."

I decided to investigate further and reached out through email to the clinic in Barbados. The more I learned, the more I liked, including their stated commitment to holistic care. From what I read, the doctors and nurses took the time to understand the individual's needs and goals, and they developed a treatment plan that was tailored to each person. It certainly seemed like you would feel like an actual woman instead of patient number whatever.

Then, there was the real moment of truth in my research. It was the moment I learned that the doctors at the clinic were all women—women who understood the intricacies of our bodies, our feelings, and our relationships with our own physical selves. These women hailed from different countries, varied in their cultural backgrounds, and proudly represented women of color—something I didn't see in the other clinics I went to.

The prevailing attitude online (if you can call it that) was that the clinic was one of pure compassion and care. They welcomed patients with open arms, urging them to leave their worries and stresses at the door. Their focus was on overall health and wellness, with equal emphasis placed on patients' emotional, mental, and spiritual well-being and physical health. For the first time in what felt like an eternity, a small glimmer of hope flickered to life within me. The idea that a medical practice could prioritize my whole self, not just my uterus (or old uterus like some doctors thought), felt like a breath of fresh air in a world that often feels indifferent to our struggles. *I bet no one would call me 'old' there!*

So, when I saw those words, "Click Here to Sign Up for a Free Consultation," I was ready, but my finger hovered over the mouse for a few seconds. There was an instant feeling of eager anticipation, but I wanted to see that sticker price before I could completely give in.

I didn't want to go through that again. Still, my eagerness won out.

Click. Data input and complete. Check!

Whew! Here I go again. "Now I just have to tell Johnnie," I whispered to myself.

Maybe I won't tell him just yet, I thought at first. I should do the consult myself and see if it sounds any good. I wouldn't want to drag Johnnie through all my drama again if it was another disappointment. I could at least spare him that.

When I got the email confirming my consultation date and time, it ended with the words—*We look forward to speaking with you and Johnnie*. I felt my heart race. *Could I really try this all again?* I wondered. *What was I thinking, making an appointment with a clinic—that's not even in this country—and not telling Johnnie about it?*

For days, I went back and forth on my decisions. I played multiple scenes out in my mind, trying to picture what might happen if I told him. It made me realize something. As a couple, Johnnie and I prided ourselves on being great communicators with each other. Keeping something from him— especially something so important—was not an example of that at all. Somehow thinking that I would protect his feelings by keeping him out of the loop wasn't sitting well with me anymore. His feelings would be hurt more if he found out I'd excluded him from the decision-making process.

Honestly, I wasn't trying to hurt him. I was scared and wanted to hear what the clinic had to say. I wanted to have hope.

Taking a deep breath, I took him aside one afternoon and slowly and hesitantly told him about this clinic my father had turned me on to and how promising they looked.

Johnnie immediately had the same reaction I first had. "No way. I'm not leaving the country for something this big. That's scary!"

"Yeah, it is," I said. Wanting him to know that I agreed with that point wholeheartedly.

"I think YOU should review them first before ruling them out though. I will email you the links to the clinic. Then see what you think. And we can talk about it," I said calmly.

Over the coming hours and days, just like my father had nagged me before, I began nagging Johnnie (like father, like daughter, I guess).

"Did you research it? What do you think? Haven't you looked at it yet? You should really look at it...."

Johnnie was dragging his feet—just like I had. And the thing was, I completely understood why he was dragging. I had been the exact same way. I don't know what made him finally go through the links I sent, but he did. And when he came across all the positive reviews for the clinic, he grew even more suspicious.

"Don't you think it's questionable that they don't have one critical review?" he asked.

"Yeah, it is. We should ask them about that."

Johnnie looked me up and down momentarily, nodding his head slightly. Then, after taking a deep breath, he said, "I think you're right."

"Great," I said swiftly.

"Because I already booked the consult. It's tomorrow at 9:00 a.m. We will get a phone call."

Johnnie tilted his head and flashed me an 'of course, you did' expression. I smiled, smacked a kiss on him, and asked him if he wanted a glass of wine. I was hoping he didn't process that I had already gone ahead with this all before speaking with him.

I was basking in it once again.

Chapter 10

Tsunami of Emotions

The day before the big ring-a-ling, the same day Johnnie got onboard with my new plan, I received an email much like an angelic message from the heavens. It was an introduction to the friendly main nurse coordinator, who would provide support and answer my burning questions. It laid out some answers for my concerns, treatment options and the financial factor that I was holding my breath for.

One topic was about stress, my old frenemy—like that uninvited guest who overstays their welcome at every party. What I didn't realize during my DIY infertility education was that stress could be one of the masterminds behind most infertility issues. It sneaks in like a stealthy ninja and wreaks havoc on your body's baby-making abilities, taking matters from bad to worse without us even realizing it.

"Many studies have shown that stress has a huge negative impact on both fertility and IVF success rates," the email read. And I thought—*Well, holy stress balls! Stress might be the villain here!*

Now, I'd like to think of myself as a logical person. I know life comes with its fair share of stress packages, courtesy of work, relationships, family, friends, and the list goes on. But could it really be that all this everyday stress was conspiring to put my baby-making plans on hold?

I found myself in a whirlwind of introspection, Sherlock Holmes'ing the origins of my stress. *Was it because I had this uncontrollable urge to micromanage every single detail of my existence, from my daily routine to planning my trips and even coordinating events that were as complex as a Rubik's Cube on steroids? Did I over stress myself with having grand expectations of a doctor who secretly possessed medical knowledge but also lacked the empathy and comfort levels of a thousand dogs? Did I stress out about our financial status and knowing we would not have enough to make a baby? Or was this stress from way before that?*

The email had an actual answer to this stress conundrum that I did not even know I needed. They dished out an entire menu of stress-busting techniques, as if they were a spa for the soul. There was massage therapy, promising pain relief, improved circulation, and stress reduction. Acupuncture was on the list too, ready to relieve pain, improve mood, and zap stress away. Reflexology promised to give my organs and systems a little pep talk. Meditation was there, all Zen-like, ready to kick stress to the curb and boost my mood. And Reiki (Japanese technique for stress reduction and relaxation using the power of touch healing and relaxation). It was like they believed in the body's very own "Avengers" team, where every part worked together for the greater good.

Interestingly, they weren't trying to sell me a time share; this was all free information. This was completely unlike my previous clinic visits, where they'd ring me up just to remind me of my appointment time and date, and heaven forbid if I dared to cancel or miss one, there'd be a fee for that too! I was so mind-blown and stress-punched, realizing that this clinic wasn't just about making babies; it was about helping me reclaim my long-lost sanity.

The email also talked about another weird three letter word, which I added to the list of things I didn't know. They stated they were JCI accredited—or, as I now like to call it, the fanciest gold star! JCI stands for Joint Commission International, and it's like the golden ticket of quality and safety for fertility clinics. These clinics don't just slap on a "trust us" sticker—they go through a rigorous evaluation process to prove they're the cream of the crop. As I (you guessed it) Googled it, I learned even more. This certification meant improved patient safety, staffing, and training. Clinics must have qualified and well-trained staff, up to date facilities and equipment, and must maintain accurate and up-to-date records.

I also learned that in the bustling world of U.S. healthcare, there was a notable absence of accreditation. As I delved into this peculiar reality, a question nagged at my soul: *Why? Why didn't U.S. healthcare organizations require this prestigious accreditation, ensuring quality of care, patient satisfaction, and a competitive edge?*

As I stared at my screen, taking it all in, I couldn't help but again feel disappointed. I realized that I wasn't an "isolated incident." This was the reality for countless women embarking on the journey to build a family. I knew all too well how we are left navigating a sea of uncertainty, hoping for the best, but not always receiving the standard of care and safety we deserved. I saw it firsthand.

The excitement of a fully loaded email of possibilities, chock-full of information that was, wait for it, FREE, was too much to take! Then, I continued to read about flying to Barbados for ultrasound monitoring, egg collection, and the embryo transfer.

Amid the whirlwind of excitement and freebies, I couldn't shake that nagging feeling of dread about the whole "going out of the country" thing. So, what did I do? I Googled. And boy, did I Google like my life depended on it. I was searching for answers like a detective on a caffeine high.

There I sat, eyes glued to the screen, yelling at our healthcare system. "Why don't you make sense? Why can't you be more like this one?" But lurking beneath all that righteous indignation was a deep fear—a fear of venturing into the unknown.

The email ended with explaining that I would need to undergo a pre-screening test. Some I had already had. Once they review it, and we have agreed to go down this road of IVF, we could then begin. "Once we receive these," the email said, "we can work toward booking your free" (This word 'Free' made me get butterflies in my stomach) "medical telephone consultation with one of our Specialist Physicians."

They continued to say, "We know that IVF is a serious issue. However, this does not mean it has to be stressful for couples."

The morning of the call. I got up dressed up as if going to a doctor's appointment, hair and makeup done too. Funny this was a phone call, but I had to feel good and that meant getting dressed.

My phone screen erupted in a frenzy of flashing lights, all thanks to an unfamiliar number. I could practically feel my heart doing somersaults in my chest, not just because we had meticulously scheduled this call, but also because I was secretly sending out telepathic messages to the universe, pleading for it not to be a telemarketer.

And then, as if the phone itself had taken a deep breath, a voice, rich with anticipation and a touch of intrigue, spoke on the other end of the line.

"Hello! My name is Dr. Jones, am I speaking with Mrs. Mandy and Mr. Johnnie Refvik?"

Her lilting Irish accent was like music to my ears, and it felt like a fairy godmother had come to grant my every wish. She used endearing terms of affection, calling us "darling," "sweetie," "Mr. Johnnie," and "Mrs. Mandy." Her voice was soothing.

After the exchange of pleasantries and a brief overview of the clinic's offerings, the inquisitive doctor got down to business.

The questions flowed like a well-rehearsed script that still felt authentic and individualized, each one a piece of the puzzle in my fertility journey. She asked the same typical questions the previous doctors asked, but then went further. Like how long we were trying? Did I have any medical conditions? She asked questions about my previous labs and if I had a regular menstrual cycle or was taking any supplements. She asked about my family history of fertility issues or genetic disorders and if I worked in high stress environments. She made sure no stone was unturned. To say she was thorough would be a huge understatement. She was also kind and empathetic. She took her time with each question and response.

She then explained they had tests, bloodwork, and scans that could help us know more about our situation. I fell in love with her right then and there. If I hadn't already been married to my husband, I might have just dropped down and proposed to her (hopefully she would say yes after the first ask). She offered me something. I couldn't put my finger on it, but it was something I could feel in my soul.

I could see in Johnnie's face that he felt the same (not that he wanted to marry her or anything, but he was impressed). He leaned over and whispered, "This feels different." The previous doctors we talked to made us feel like we were on a baby making assembly line.

That flicker of hope turned into an all-out wildfire at that moment. She talked briefly about our other options too, like adoption and surrogacy. She was honest—IVF didn't have a 100% guarantee—but she didn't dwell on the impossibility of it either.

As I continued to bathe in the soothing sound of her voice, I found that annoying thought from that previous doctor entering my mind. And I couldn't let it go. She was starting to wrap up and asked, "Any questions for me?" I jumped on the opportunity and blurted out like a toddler on sugar, "Yes! You know, since I am ancient to these U.S. doctors, and now I am about to turn 40, do you think I have a chance to still have children?" I had to hear what she had to say.

I heard her give a sigh and I immediately put my head down. She approached the subject with compassion and understanding. I'm sure she could gather that it was a sensitive topic for me, and she went on to explain to me that women are born with a certain number of eggs. As a fetus early in development, a baby with ovaries has around six million eggs. I couldn't help but think—*That's some seriously impressive inventory management!* The number of these eggs is reduced to between one and two million by the time we are born. Then, as we age, that number can decrease dramatically, causing difficulties in the journey toward conception.

She didn't say, "Yes" or "No, you're too old." She calmed my nerves by reassuring me that these "speed bumps" like my age and reduction of eggs, along with my endometriosis there could still be a possibility. She was the first doctor to feel that my endometriosis was something to look into as well. Whereas the other doctor said it was nothing to worry about.

"Let's put together a plan," she said.

What a contrasted difference, in approach, and in diagnosis. I was being addressed as a whole person, not a uterus on legs and not someone who was 'too old' to have children. I was a person. I was a woman. Not a non-white woman. Not an old woman. A woman.

As soon as that telephone chat wrapped up, I was hit with a tsunami of emotions—and let me tell you, it was a full-blown spectacle. Tears and more tears. My waterworks show outlasted the length of the phone call itself, which had been about 40 minutes long. But my emotional breakdown? That thing was in it for the long haul.

I was sitting there with eyes all puffy and red, staring at Johnnie, who was looking at me. He reached over, gave me a hug, and said, "I'm glad we didn't throw in the towel. Flying to another country still gives me an uneasy feeling, but that lady on the phone? Total pro. Let's just hope the price doesn't have too many zeros after it."

I nodded, still a teary mess, and agreed. Soon after, I got another email with attachments. One was a questionnaire, the basic intake questionnaire you would complete when you got to any doctor's office, and then a test requisition with a list of tests that needed to be completed. More tests—no problem!

For the next two weeks, Johnnie and I each seemed to be in a certain state of disbelief. We needed some time to process this. *Were we about to embark on something this crazy? Was it crazy? Were we really ready for this? From just one phone call and some Google searching?* But no matter how "crazy" it seemed, it also seemed right.

We were going down this path, and despite any fears or reluctance, I could not wait!

Chapter 11

Homework and Hurdles

While we continued to rack our brains about going abroad for a medical procedure, I tried to maintain my logical sense of what came next. I was focusing on the tests that were being requested. And of course, good old Google was going to be my companion. *What were these tests and why were they so important?*

The clinic requested the following tests—an Antibody, a Full Blood Count, Anti-Mullerian Hormone (AMH), Antiphospholipid (aPLs), Anti Thyroglobulin Antibody (TgAb), Anti Microsomal Antibody (AMA), two diagnostic tests, a smear test, an Salin Infusion Sonogram (SIS), and a transvaginal ultrasound to assess my endometrial lining thickness and ovarian follicle number and measurements.

My fertility knowledge continued to grow. I learned that the AMH is a blood test to assess your ovarian reserve. The aPLs blood test is particularly for women who are dealing with infertility and recurrent miscarriages. In addition to a Thyroid-Stimulating Hormone (TSH) test which is crucial for fertility for multiple reasons because the thyroid gland plays a vital role in the regulation of hormones throughout the body. And I found out about Prolactin, and its role in regulating various aspects of the reproductive system.

Going further, I found out that blood group compatibility between partners can be a consideration treatment. If a woman has Rh-negative blood and her partner has Rh-positive blood, there may be a risk of Rh incompatibility in the baby. This is particularly important during pregnancy but can also be relevant in fertility treatments that involve assisted reproductive techniques.

A day later, another email came in from the clinic's financial aid department. This email came as a financial breakdown for the process. It itemized the procedures, process, and medication, which included IVF-ICSI Cycle, blastocyst, pre-genetic screening, and medication. Johnnie and I sat at the kitchen table and began pouring over the pamphlets from the previous doctors versus this one from overseas. We played music and popped open a bottle of wine. Johnnie brought out the old school calculator, added a pencil behind his ear, and began dancing around. I began calculating costs on his outdated calculator, but my numbers kept coming up differently every time.

I started to get frustrated and in the typical Johnnie manner he said, "Hey, hey, hey, come here, I can do it for you." He then whipped out his cellphone to the calculator app and began punching away. As I looked over, I began laughing. I asked, "Why do we have a calculator and a pencil when we can clearly do the calculations on our cellphone?"

He began laughing, "I was just trying to get into the character of a CPA, but I have no idea what you are doing."

This made me begin to laugh as well, lightening the mood instantly. *Could we really afford this?* The U.S. doctors made it clear we could expect the IVF process to cost upwards of $50,000. But at the Barbados Fertility Clinic, it was significantly less, to the tune of $12,000. And they only wanted a quarter down! Like $3,000! *We could do that.*

We reviewed spreadsheets, handwritten notes, and our printed-out research.

For hours, we furiously sorted and organized the information. We each came up with our pros and cons list.

We went over the cost of the medications, necessary travel and lodging, various procedures, including pre-genetic screening and blastocyst, sedatives, retrieval, and the extraction of the eggs, and more, which was not included in the initial costs. Finally, we calculated all the costs to be around $14,000. That figure felt comfortable. It would still be a challenge, but we could do this! Yes, it was still a lot of money, but this was possible.

Our pros side of the page was much longer than our cons with everything from information, education, expertise, and financials, but still, the travel notion was lingering. Finally, we called it a night, more content than uneasy.

The next morning, I got another informative email with a nice step-by-step process. This was music to my ears! I am a planner, so having a checklist to check off was my happy place. Either Santa or the clinic was listening to my wants, and I was all for it.

The email looked like this.

<u>YOUR IVF CYCLE TIMELINE (Int'l)</u>

STEP 1: Contact us via email, phone, or fax to set up an initial Telephone Consultation with our Consultant Physician. CHECK!

STEP 2: A Phone Consultation with our Physician. At this appointment, your full medical and fertility history will be reviewed. If IVF is the treatment plan determined for you, you will be scheduled for a phone consultation with one of our IVF Nurse Coordinators. CHECK!

STEP 3: A phone consultation with an *IVF Nurse Coordinator*. Your nurse will discuss with you any Pre-cycle lab tests that need to be performed prior to a cycle.

You will be guided through what your IVF cycle will entail. Also, a timeframe will be discussed that will best accommodate suitable dates for your IVF cycle and travel plans. CHECK and CHECK!

STEP 4: A phone consultation or email from our Financial Coordinator. This appointment is to discuss what your overall cost will be and what the financial package includes.

 CHECK! (and here is my check!)

STEP 5: Complete your pre-cycle lab tests. We will work with your GP, local Doctor, or Consultant Gynaecologist to perform these so your cycle can commence.

These tests include hormonal, immunological, and screening blood tests for the female partner and a uterine evaluation. The tests needed for the male partner include infectious screening blood tests and a recent Semen Analysis.

Okay. This is easy peasy, I thought. Off to the gyno's office so I can add a check mark to this part of the list, and I can complete all my steps!

On the morning of my appointment, I woke up feeling great. I was ready to take on the day, and figured the appointment would be a piece of cake. I was singing out loud, dancing in my car, window down—great kind of morning! I felt positive for the first time in a long time. I'm not the most upbeat person on a normal day, but today's doctor's appointment was going to be good. The Barbados clinic had really altered my perception of things and had me thinking everything was going to be ok.

"Good morning," the receptionist said, without a smile, when I walked in.

"I am here for my 9:00 a.m. appt with Dr. Dennis," I replied.

"Have a seat," the not-so-pleasant receptionist said to me. I brushed it off. *You're not going to take my joy away!*

After over an hour in the waiting room, which consisted of three refreshes on Facebook, playing solitaire, and browsing through three parents and baby magazines on the table, my patience (and positivity) was wearing thin. Although the wait annoyed me, I tried to hold onto the fact that it would all be worth it.

"Mandy," the nurse called out. *Ahh, yes, finally!*

I followed her to the exam room and got the whole spiel— "Get undressed, put this gown on, and the doctor will be with you shortly."

I did this so fast I didn't even fold my panties—just tucked them away into my other clothes. *I was ready, let's do this!*

And now more waiting, but in an annoying paper robe, freezing in a white sterile room, looking at the random hair growth on my legs, digging my fingernails absentmindedly into the uncomfortable gyno-table. *What is taking this doctor so long?*

Knock, Knock

"Yes, finally," I muttered.

"Come in," I said more loudly, so they could hear on the other side of the door.

Dr. Dennis, a petite white lady with red hair and an oversized lab jacket, entered the room.

"Ok, Mandy, looks like you are up to date on your pap. What are you in for?"

"Yes, so I am going to Barbados to do IVF, and I need these labs done. They need it in advance. I am planning on going in a few weeks."

She looked it over, walked over to her laptop, typed something up, turned to me, and said, "I can only perform the HIV and Hep test. Your insurance won't cover the rest."

I slowly took the paper from her outstretched hand and looked at it again. I looked up at her with a confused look on my face.

"You can't do an AMH, aPLs, or TgAb test," I asked her, rattling out acronyms as if I were a pro.

"No," she replied quickly.

"But you're my OB/GYN and these are all for my ovarian and fertility health. That's you," I said, with very much of an attitude.

This is probably why she closed the laptop and walked toward the door.

"Well, all I can do are those two. If you want them, I will send the nurse in."

I had to think for a split minute. "Yes, I will get it done." I obviously had no other options.

As I watched her leave without a polite goodbye or any further explanation, my heart ached. I felt confused. My eyes felt like they were in rapid response time, looking from left to right, trying to figure out what to do next. As the nurse entered, I thought I could ask her where I could get these labs done or how much it would cost out of pocket, but I hesitated. *Out of pocket? WTF? Why should I pay for bloodwork out of pocket?* I sat there watching her take blood and felt my heartbeat going faster and faster.

The nurse turned to me and asked, "Are you ok?"

This was my opportunity to speak up.

"Ahem, how much will these labs cost out of pocket? I pointed to the piece of paper in my hand. The doctor said my insurance won't cover them."

"Let me see," she said, as she walked over to her laptop, "Well, I can't really see the full price, but I am guessing your AMA may be about $5,000 and the same for all the others. As for the smear test, you can use your pap smear, but you would have to pay out of pocket because you already had one this year," the nurse said in a little dismal voice.

My eyes began to tear up. I waited for the nurse to be done and walk out the door. I quickly got off the table, got dressed, and ran out of the doctor's office faster than I ever thought possible. I panic-walked to my car, got in, and drove home feeling stressed and anxious. I felt deflated … again! I was no longer happy and energized. I was confused. *What just happened?*

I had to remind myself—*Don't go into this funk again. We will find another doctor.* I immediately sat at my desk and called my insurance company and multiple doctors looking for someone to run these simple labs for me for weeks.

And these calls only bolstered my disgusted thoughts about navigating the U.S. healthcare system while seeking fertility treatment.

Not only is it hard to know the difference between an OB/GYN, REI (Reproductive Endocrinology and Infertility), or a PCP, you must figure out the insurance shit on top of it all.

In all honesty, my mind raced with the many "whys." *Why would an OB/GYN not do those tests for me? That is a doctor specializing in female reproductive health, pregnancy, and childbirth. So, why am I having difficulty finding a doctor to perform these tests? Is it the doctor? Is it the insurance company? Is it me?*

I ran into countless obstacles. I found one doctor who could see me. When I got there, she told me she couldn't do the tests because she didn't believe in IVF. I couldn't wrap my mind around that one—how a female doctor, and a doctor for women's health, would deny me the chance to get pregnant. Was it even legal to be denied health care when I had written requests from another doctor to have those tests done?

Inadequacy crept in with this endless game of telephone. *Was it me? Was I asking the wrong questions? What was I doing wrong?*

I called countless other clinics. They were all resistant.

"Well fuck!" I screamed after every phone call.

Chapter 12

Checklist Chronicles

I had *not* expected this horrible setback. It made me sick. Or something did! Because later that week, I found myself in urgent care. I sat in the waiting room, angry. I was back to being annoyed and harboring an extreme dislike for doctors. The Barbados doctor must have put a spell on me, making me think that doctors could have your back. But it just wasn't true. I was at the end of my friggin' rope. So, when the urgent care doctor, slim in frame, her hair in a high bun, confident and comfortable, dressed in grey slacks and white sneakers asked me "Are you pregnant?" after the nurses had already asked once, I completely lost it.

I couldn't help glaring at her and then barked vehemently, as if it were her fault: "No! No, I'm not. I'm *trying* to, but YOU doctors don't want to help me."

As I laid on the table, hating the world and the bright lights that seem to have me under a magnifying glass. Every bottled-up emotion bursted out of me. I wanted to cry and scream. I was just so pissed!

She stepped back slightly, with a bit of an attitude, but must have recognized my emotional pain because she remarked, "What do you mean?"

I exhaled through the tears that started streaming down my face, while shaking, "I have a script to get labs done so I can have a baby. And all the doctors I have gone to and called will not help me. I don't know what else to do." I opened my purse, which had the folded-up prescription from after the first doctor's let down appointment.

"See now it is crushed down, just like I am," I cried.

"Can I see that?" The doctor asked.

I looked at her and tried to iron out the wrinkled script and handed it to her. She looked over it and said, "Oh, I can send those out. That's easy."

I was stunned. "You *can?*"

"Yeah. I can do some right now actually. We would have the results in a couple of days."

I just looked at her and began sobbing uncontrollably, which was followed by a snot trail and a deep, guttural cough, followed by a loud fart.

"I don't know what the fuck is wrong with me, but you just possibly made my dreams come true."

She then chuckled, which turned the snarky atmosphere in the room to laughter.

"But, for this blood panel," she said, pointing to one of the lab requests on my list, "you'll need to be fasting. That means no breakfast and coming in early. If you don't come in early…" she began.

"Oh, don't you worry," I cut her off. "I'll be here!"

I understood her tone and didn't care that she gave me a little funny attitude. All I needed from her were those labs. It bewildered me that a doctor in urgent care could run them and have them to me in two days. And all I could think was—*I am not crazy! There is a fundamental problem in our healthcare system. But right now, I need to worry about me and getting my baby! It just should not be so fucking difficult.*

As it turns out, I only had a cold, but the universe brought me exactly where I needed to be that day. *So amazing, right?*

As promised, my labs were ready in two days and were finally being sent off to Barbados Fertility Clinic (BFC). All I could do was wait and wait some more and then anxiously wait for the doctor to make her assessment and tell me what the next steps would be.

Three days of biting my nails and going over all the scenarios in my head, like—*What if they say I see no baby in your future? Or your eggs that looked great two years ago and don't anymore?* The worst thoughts came piling in.

I went back to the urgent care for the ultrasound and blood test that I had needed to fast for. The same doctor was there, and she was wonderful. I quickly realized that she was much more than a doctor—she was an angel in disguise. I will always keep a special place in my heart for her.

On the fifth day of waiting, that familiar ding sound came through. I received an email from BFC asking me to schedule a call with them. They suggested I continue to take my prenatal, vitamin C, D, folic acid, CoQ10, and birth control pills. *Wait, what? I had to take birth control pills to get pregnant. Now I really felt like I was losing my mind.*

Still, I trusted them and if they told me to take something, I was taking it! The labs were done, and the clinic wants to talk. Two more checks off the list. We were moving in the right direction.

STEP 6: Coordination of your IVF cycle. Once these tests are completed, your IVF cycle can begin. The cycle is commenced by starting the birth control pill. This is to commence the down regulation of the ovaries and gives us the ability to schedule your cycle and travel dates in advance.

Okay, if they say so. CHECK and CHECK!

I scheduled the call for the next day. I was too excited to wait for weeks to discuss what they found out. We needed to start now! I was fully engaged in this process. As for Johnnie, he wasn't entirely convinced, but I think my motivation to keep going kept him quiet.

The phone rang, and my heart started racing with excitement. I answered, eager to hear the news, hurrying Johnnie up to sit in on the call. On the other line was the sweet accent I only heard once and was excited to hear again. I imagined her saying "You will be pregnant by Christmas, picture a Christmas baby." *I mean if that isn't a hallmark Christmas movie then I don't know what is.* The pleasantries were there, and she seemed to want to get right into the conversation, saying she saw a few polyps on my last ultrasound—five polyps, to be exact.

"Polyps?" I asked. I had no idea what that was. I looked over at Johnnie to see if he knew and he just shrugged his shoulders.

"What do polyps do and what does it mean for getting pregnant," I asked.

She told me that the growth rate of polyps in a woman's body can vary depending on the type of polyp, as well as other individual factors such as age and overall health and they can take several years to grow to full size. Hyperplastic polyps are slow-growing and may take years or decades to develop. Some types of polyps, such as adenomatous polyps, can grow more quickly and may reach a detectable size in a shorter period.

She told me that these looked like they had been growing for a few years based on their size. *WTF—a few years? What did this mean? Was this the issue of why I never got pregnant? I couldn't believe it!* I had visited my regular OB/GYN yearly for pap smears, and three different fertility clinics and none had ever said that they saw any issues.

Her suggestion at this point was to speak with my OB/GYN and or an REI specialist who specializes in the diagnosis and treatment of infertility and other reproductive disorders. This was a defining moment for me.

I no longer wanted to go to my OB because of her lack of interest in me having a baby. I knew I had to be my own advocate for my health, my life, and my family.

As I tried to process the news that I had polyps on my uterus, my mind raced with questions and fears. *What if the polyps had destroyed all my possibilities? What if the medications worked, and we had gotten pregnant, only to have our hopes and dreams dashed by these benign growths?* The thought of these polyps interfering with our ability to carry a child was devastating. It felt like we had been dealt yet another blow on our already tiresome journey toward parenthood. The impact this could have on our future family felt exhausting just thinking about it.

As the reality of the situation set in, I couldn't help but feel overwhelmed by a sense of frustration and helplessness. I could not control these growths in my body, of course. So, what do I do now?

Now it was back to the drawing board of looking for an OB/GYN or an REI—someone who could look at these scans and tell me what to do so I could get back on track with having a baby. I learned the hard way about how to go about finding doctors and having tests done in the past, so I was going to call my insurance company to help me find a specialist who took my insurance.

What came after was even more disturbing, though. Another round of phone calls and dead-end doctors. So, there I was, embarking on the quest to find a doctor willing to play magician with my reproductive bits, and guess what?

"We are not accepting new patients right now."

"The next appointment we have available is next year."

"We no longer accept your insurance."

These were the answers I was getting when calling multiple doctor's offices. It was exhausting.

It took three weeks, but I finally got an appointment with a doctor who worked with my insurance.

This doctor was an Obstetrician, whose office was twelve miles from where I lived. The office was small, the waiting room was crowded, the walls were yellow with posters and printed out papers taped to them. The ceiling had that awkward lighting with some bulbs flickering on and off. Some of the panels seemed like they had water damage. The women behind the thick bullet proof type glass seemed uninterested in who was standing in front of them. I waited there patiently and observed all that was happening in the office, looking around to all the women sitting there. I wondered why they were all there. *Do we all have the same problem? Is this doctor worth the wait?* He wasn't my first choice or even second. He didn't even have any raving reviews from other patients. But I needed to see someone fast.

I was given a clipboard with some papers and told to have a seat. My wait was about an hour and a half. I sat. I stood. I walked around. I looked out the window. I called my mom. I called my dad. I called any friend who had time to chat. I called Johnnie about 20 times.

I was relieved that Johnnie couldn't make it with me to this appointment as I knew he wouldn't have liked it any more than I did.

Finally, my name got butchered by the nurse, who seemed tired and annoyed. I popped up and followed her through the yellow-walled office. I was welcomed by the doctor who seemed to have been waiting for me already. I have never been to an office where the doctor is in the room before I was. This felt off. He had my files in his hands and was ready to begin.

This older gentleman (let's call him Dr. Hyde) had good humor and did a thorough review of my labs and folder. He had read all the items I listed on the documents. I was impressed. It made me think if he is like this to me, then he may be doing this for others, which is why he was so behind on schedule. I honestly couldn't get mad at that.

We spoke at length, and he provided me a full detail of what my polyps looked like and how they could attribute to my fertility issues.

He suggested we remove them. I was not excited about surgery, but if this meant we could have a clean slate, then I was all for it.

"But before we do that, we would need to check with your insurance company to see what they will cover," he said.

"But isn't this something that I need?" I asked.

"In my opinion, Yes! Let's just confirm to make sure there aren't any out-of-pocket expenses, and I'm sure if there are, they will be minor."

Based on what he said, I felt encouraged and that he was looking out for my financial wellbeing as well. I left his office expecting a positive phone call and a date for surgery.

The wait began. I sat there wondering if they had forgotten about me. After three days, I decided I would let their office get settled and then call at 9:30 a.m. but they beat me to it. I got a call from the nurse telling me my insurance wouldn't pay for the procedure to remove my uterine polyps.

My insurance company deemed them unnecessary to remove because they were not "harmful" to my health. *I mean, isn't that fucking ridiculous?*

I was livid! There was a potential that this could impact my fertility and disrupt my body's balance. The anger and frustration I felt were almost overwhelming.

It was bad enough that I had to deal with the emotional toll of struggling to conceive. Now I had to deal with insurance companies denying me the medical care I needed to make my dream of starting a family a reality. It felt like a slap in the face.

I wanted nothing more than to have a baby, and here they were telling me that my health and my choices didn't matter. Who were they to cherry-pick who could or could not have a baby? Or who could have foreign growths removed from their bodies?

While I was wondering what I would do next, I got another phone call from the same nurse within a few minutes. She said the doctor could still do the procedure and it would be covered.

There was a way. It was medically necessary because of *blah blah blah*. I honestly didn't care what else they had to say.

Not only was I set back on my timeline *again*, but I was bargain shopping for my uterus. *Again.*

Great!

I was told not to stress by the clinic. But how could I avoid being stressed? This entire process was one stressor layered on top of another!

One day, I decided I was not working at all. I was not going to Google either. I was going to do nothing else other than lie in bed. I began to channel surf, all the shows that paused in front of me were shows like "Botched," "The Knick," and "Nurse Jackie." Watching show after show about the wrong doctor terrified me. I knew I would be fucked if I didn't find a good doctor to remove the polyps correctly and keep my uterus safe. And I began to pause—*Was this Doctor Hyde a good decision?*

The surgery I needed posed its very own risk. I didn't know how big the polyps were, if they had caused any damage to my uterus, or what they could have done to my other reproductive organs. There wasn't a test for that. Having surgery on that part of my abdomen could also have adverse effects on my chances of conceiving and carrying to term. A huge kick in the nuts (not that I had to worry about that body part!).

The surgery date was set, and fear engulfed me. On the day of the surgery, it was overwhelming. Butterflies again started fluttering around. We finally got called into the pre-surgical room. There were many nurses walking around, and doctors with scrubs on. Machines were beeping.

The doctor came in after my IV was inserted, and monitors were placed in position. The doctor explained the procedure and told me there was no set time frame for recovery. It would take a while.

I feared recovery the most, especially after I learned polyps could regrow even after removing them.

Well, fuck me again!

By then, I thought I must be the walking model of fucking insanity. Doing the same thing and expecting a different result. *Why, why did I sign up for this cluster fuck of emotional distress?*

I gave Johnnie a kiss and was fast asleep in seconds.

Chapter 13

Ankle Woes and Fiscal Prose

The surgery was a success. Now it was just time to wait for the healing. For days after, I couldn't walk, not just because I was on bedrest, but also because I had twisted my ankle.

In the month-long wait it had taken to get an appointment for the surgery, I was incredibly emotional. In that time, I had about seven emotional breakdowns, including three arguments with Johnnie about things from what to eat for dinner to him not understanding why I was so emotional. And I honestly didn't know why I was so emotional. Could it have been from the birth control meds, the setback of schedule, or the fact that I was closer to the process? One night, I decided it was okay to let myself go and socialize and get out of my own head. After a few too many cocktails and ugly crying to a friend about this fertility journey, as well as a bit of husband bashing, we walked out of the restaurant laughing and hugging, and I overstepped the sidewalk. Down I went. I mean, talk about adding insult to injury (literally)! My body was like, "Can we please catch a break here?"

So, as I laid in bed in a bathrobe, with pain in my abdomen and ankle. I used Yelp to research doctors because I had no other options at the time. I am aware that there are some very needy patients out there, so I judged based on how the reviews were worded. Dr. Hyde reviews did talk about the long wait, which I attributed to an impatient patient, and they were completely right on that one. But as for his knowledge and bedside manner, he was incredible. The other reviewers said he was rude and lazy. I felt the complete opposite. I appreciated his honesty, knowledge, and care, which made me feel the most comfortable.

And his aftercare was also very comforting. He called to see how I was feeling, and he wished me best wishes on my baby journey.

He also provided suggestions on vitamins and foods to eat from his culture to help with having a baby. This doctor also, made it a priority to let the insurance company know this was a necessary procedure.

As we waited for my follow-up appointment, Johnnie and I went back and forth about our finances. We discussed using our savings and what that would mean. We talked about Johnnie's next project and how much he could possibly make, but it wasn't clear how long the project would go on, and if this client would follow through on the 60-day terms. In the construction world, there is always a longer wait time on payment, which is unfortunate (not to mention, making it difficult to plan anything). We talked about it every night at dinner. The money made us nervous. Even though $14,000 was more comfortable than $50,000, it was still a pretty big number. What if we spent all that money and it didn't work? What happens if we need to do another round? Were we okay with one round?

A week later, we were on one of our calls with my parents on WhatsApp. Johnnie and I revealed to them that we chose BFC to do the process, but that we might need to hold off because although the price wasn't that bad, we had just hit a snag with our finances. I knew we sounded down on our call, and my parents asked us if we had any other options financially. We told them what we mapped out exactly but were still not sure. My parents went silent for a while, as if they were thinking of how to say something. The pause made me look at the phone to see if they had frozen because of the Wi-Fi, but then my dad spoke up.

"Your mom and I were talking, and we want to help you guys with this," he said, while my mom nodded enthusiastically.

"Help us with what?" I asked.

"We want to give you guys the money to try and have a baby."

Johnnie, being the prideful person he is, refused to accept their generosity. "Hey pops, as much as that sounds great, we don't know the foreseeable future and I can't, we can't accept that. But we thank you," Johnnie said.

I was in shock they would offer us so much money, but deep down, I felt excited because this was a huge stress that could be removed very quickly. But after I heard Johnnie speak up, I thought he was right too. I couldn't say anything in that moment as I struggled to navigate my emotions. I just stayed quiet and listened to my father and Johnnie go back and forth.

"Let's call it a loan and you pay it back if you don't have a baby," my father said.

I mean, we already bargain-shopped for polyp removal and having a baby, what's wrong with taking out a loan on top of all of it? If this wasn't an indicator of the two amazing grandparents, I didn't know what was, and it would be an amazing story to tell our child.

I remember Johnnie looking over at me and then looking back at my father on the screen. "Let us talk it over and we will let you know," he said. "We thank you for that offer as well. That could change everything for us."

In the haze of shock, I clung to the illusion that we could bear the weight of our struggles alone. Like a solitary hero in a personal saga, I held onto the idea that we could shoulder the burden without burdening others. It was almost comical, looking back, how we convinced ourselves that we had to be the lone warrior in this battle.

Then, unexpectedly, my parents stepped in with this offer that shattered my self-imposed isolation. My initial reaction was a mix of disbelief and gratitude. It wasn't just about the financial aid (when you're proud it hurts to ask for it), but it was about the courage to accept help, to acknowledge that vulnerability doesn't diminish strength but enhances it. It's a quirky twist of fate that sometimes the bravest thing you can do is not to face everything alone.

Johnnie and I deliberated for days about accepting financial assistance from my parents. When my mom called two days later, offering again, I expressed that we hadn't reached a decision yet.

Secretly, I was inclined to scream *"Yes!"* at the top of my lungs, but Johnnie didn't match my energy. While he didn't explicitly articulate his reservations, I understood that he'd always prided himself on achieving everything through hard work, without external assistance. It was a foreign concept for him. To ease his concerns, I presented various options for considering the loan.

I suggested we could make manageable, small payments to ensure it wouldn't become a burden. I even assured him that I would take charge as the intermediary with my parents, addressing any issues that might arise and ensuring the situation remained under control, all in hopes that he would take the offer. I badgered him for days, all while my mom lovingly badgered me.

All during this back and forth with my parents and Johnnie, I had finally gotten that appointment for the follow-up ultrasound. A day later I received an email that came back with, "Attached is a timetable to get prepared and a list of medications. Let's schedule a call to go over everything."

I screamed out "Fuck Yes!" after seeing those words pop up onto my computer screen.

I took a deep breath and was feeling pumped. A wave of hopefulness fluttered through me. I cried a lot that day. After all the challenges we had encountered, it elated me to receive an email from the clinic informing me they were ready to start the preparations. Johnnie and I both knew it wasn't a done deal. We had a long journey ahead, with no guarantees. It was the first ounce of positivity we'd had through this entire ordeal. We also agreed to graciously accept my parents' help.

So now ... back to the original checklist.

STEP 7: After two to four weeks on the pill, your down-regulation will continue with the use of subcutaneous injection for another ten days. At this stage, down-regulation will be confirmed by an ultrasound or blood test with your own doctor so your cycle start can be commenced. Full cycle payment is due currently.

CHECK and I am writing you a CHECK!

Chapter 14

Prescription Perplexities

We were in hot pursuit. When we began this baby-making journey, little did we know all the hassles that would seemingly try to deter us. Finding the right clinic, finding a doctor for tests, finding a doctor for polyp removal. And now finding the meds that were somewhat affordable.

I held onto the hope that the road ahead would be smooth, only to realize that my assumptions were ignorant. *Honestly, I don't know why I thought anything would be smooth at all.* Although the intensity of the research had reduced, a great deal of effort was still required, which I had become quite skilled at by then.

The clinics I visited previously had provided me with a list of places outside the U.S. where I could purchase the necessary medications as they stated that the cost here was pricey. Their thought process was that since the cost of fertility was expensive, buying medications out of the U.S. would help financially. Furthermore, the shipping costs were higher than the costs of the medications themselves. I also discovered that most of the medications that were needed were not covered by insurance.

I did ample research to get these elusive medications. In my moment of despair, my father emerged as my unwavering rescuer, a modern-day knight whose armor shone with love and determination. Despite being miles away in Trinidad, he swiftly orchestrated a miracle. Knowing that the clinic in Barbados had a branch in his location, he seized the opportunity to secure the vital medications we needed. His resourcefulness not only saved us precious time but also lightened the financial burden, as the costs were more manageable there.

With unwavering dedication, he personally undertook the arduous journey to transport the medication, ensuring it reached me just in time. The weight that lifted off my shoulders was immeasurable, a testament to the boundless love and care my dad enveloped me in. I mean, who needs Amazon Prime when you've got a dad who can make transcontinental drug runs like a pro? *Am I right?* It was just another one of his many gifts to us, and we couldn't be more grateful. Who knows, we'll start a family business of international drug smuggling. *Just kidding!* But hey, in making a baby, you do what you got to do!

My medication was like a symphony of excitement and terror, all wrapped up in one Amazon-style box filled with vials, pills, and needles—*Oh, the needles!* I swear, this package had more sharp objects than a serial killer's toolkit.

There were needles of all shapes and sizes, from thin ones that looked like they could break with a gust of wind to thick ones that could make a lumberjack flinch. And don't even get me started on the injections that looked like they were meant for a horse.

I wasn't familiar with any of the names of these medicines and practically needed a magnifying glass to read that tiny 3-point font. To top it off, I was trying to make sense of the French instructions in English! No wonder the words seemed like a foreign language to me—they were! After a bit of a language treasure hunt, I finally found the English instructions. I was just so exhausted, but I needed to figure this out because I had to start my medications the very next day.

After unravelling them all, I had a compulsory need to read and review each one. I wanted comfort in what I was taking and to compare the medications with others who have experienced them. As the evening went on, I went back to my dear friend Google, and attempted to untangle the names and creators of medications. I discovered one of the shots they had prescribed was not approved here in the U.S. Still, even with my distrust of medicine and healthcare in the U.S., I got nervous anyway.

The results got bizarre! This medication called Goserelin/Zolodex is given to both men with prostate cancer and women with breast cancer and uterine disorders. *Talk about a versatile drug, right?* So, there I was, nervous, wondering if they had sent me the wrong meds. I panicked.

So, I woke up early the next morning and made the long-distance call. There was no way I was leaving it up to an email. I needed it to come directly from the mouth of the doctor.

Passing some morning pleasantries, I got right to my questions.

"Am I supposed to be taking this medication for cancer? What's going to happen if I take it? What is this supposed to do?" I asked.

I was completely shocked as the doctor explained it was all part of the plan. My head was spinning from all the medication information I reviewed the night before.

"They originally used that medication for cancer. It also works for endometriosis," the doctor confirmed.

Since I was diagnosed with endometriosis, she explained that it works to decrease the amount of estrogen in the blood and would calm the endometrium down, which is what I needed for treatment.

"Okay, okay," I mumbled. But I still didn't really understand it. I okayed her so much that I could sense she knew I was just letting her speak. She asked if I had any other questions and told me that the meds were tailored to my body and needs.

After hanging up, I was still feeling weary. I looked over at my kitchen counter, which now resembled a chemistry lab. It was time to begin my first round of shots.

The timetable was for 12 to 14 days of prepping my body for egg harvesting in BFC. I needed a whole separate calendar, planner, and alarm system to keep track of the medications and when and how I was supposed to give them to myself.

While Johnnie and I sat there looking at each of the medications and matching them with the proper dosages per the instructions, and then logging what time and when to take them, I kept chewing my lip nervously. He could see my apprehension and anxiety, as I shakily picked up the needles.

"Well, why don't you take them in the morning. Then you won't have to think about it the rest of the day and you won't be anxious about it." Johnnie said.

"Alright, I'll give that a try," I agreed.

It should have worked, in theory.

Chapter 15

Curves, Couture, and Cringes

I began a new routine …

It was time—time to begin measuring a two-part vial—a liquid and a powder.

First, the liquid had to be extracted with a syringe. Then, it needed to be added to the powder. It had to be shaken like a cocktail until it was mixed. The new mix had to be removed from the small vial with a new syringe. Then, I would change the head of the syringe with a needle to give myself the injection. This would have to be done daily. I clutched my chest, my shirt soaking through with sweat. Now time to inject. But I really couldn't.

"Just breathe. Breathe babe," Johnnie said as he watched. My hands were shaking with one holding the injection and one squeezing a small amount of fat of my stomach. Even my vision was blurry. I could feel the sweat dripping down my back and under my arms. I stood there in the kitchen just staring down at the injection. Johnnie stood there and watched me tear up as I said, "Babe, I can't do this."

"Yes, you can," he said.

"Do you want me to help you?" Johnnie asked. I looked over at him and nodded yes.

I passed the injection over to Johnnie. I took a deep breath, looked up, and let him push the needle into a small section of my stomach. I could feel the needle piercing the layers of skin.

"Babe, breathe," Johnnie directed again.

I could also feel the needle coming back out of my skin. Another tear came down when he was done. Johnnie looked at me and said, "One down, 300 more to go."

I instantly was alerted and asked, "What? I have to do 300 of them?"

Johnnie started laughing and said, "See! You're not thinking about the pain anymore!"

He was right! I reached over to swat him for scaring the shit out of me, and I began laughing, all while holding the cold pack he handed me for my stomach. Although I was done with that one, I knew I had another one to do later that evening and on and on for the next two weeks.

Day one was hard, and every day for the next two weeks was just as hard. Every time I went to bed, I felt that anxiety creep in. I'd lie awake, staring at the ceiling, sweating beneath the blankets as I thought of all the injections, I'd have to give myself when I woke up. I kept having to remind myself that we'd sought this out. It was necessary to have a baby—another step, hopefully, closer to getting what we wanted.

I started my day with one shot right in the stomach. Then, I would pop open my pill box and down six types of vitamins and meds. After that, I would pound two large glasses of water and a cup of hot tea. And next, I would stand in front of my living room window, holding a cold ice pack on my stomach and daydreaming of a child running and laughing outside. Those daydreams are exactly what got me through it all.

Then, it was time to sit at my desk, do some work, and check some emails. During lunch, there was an entirely new set of pills. And before dinner, I would run to the gym, little bit of cardio, some light weights, and walk on the treadmill for 30 minutes. Then another shot to the stomach, another cold pack, finally add some arnica (a pain reliever) to the area.

I did this for days, and I didn't feel great. But I was super optimistic. *I had this!* I was on the path that was bringing me closer to having a baby. *It was going to happen!* And then, the realization of what hormones were doing to me kicked in.

I was so consumed with the routine; I didn't realize how my attitude and emotions were changing. It was like my emotions were on a joyride, revved up higher than a marathon runner fueled by Red Bull. I started gaining weight, my skin decided it was high school prom with a breakout extravaganza, and my breasts were staging their own version of a protest—tender and sore. And as for the intimate moments with my husband, well, let's just say it felt like trying to revitalize a dry-rotted tree branch—dry as the Sahara. You asked about my sex drive? Oh, it must have taken a vacation without telling me. Of course, my naïveté and hopeful self immediately declared, "I must be pregnant!"

I was feeling something in my body in a new way. One Saturday I felt the need to have some time with my family. It was a typical day. The guys were watching some game on TV or some superhero movie, and the ladies were sitting, talking, and laughing. Out of a conversation of who knows what, my sister-in-law Cindy and I got into an argument over something trivial, so trivial that it is embarrassing to even say what it was about. But what she said to me had my emotions on a rage.

"Hey, you're overreacting and being hormonal," she said.

Steam had to be coming out of my ears. Everyone paused and watched as I lost my shit. *Who would dare say that to a hormonal woman?* I was so furious that I was ready to flip the house upside down. I was raging with emotions. She just stood there and looked at me and calmly walked away. I was standing there with no words, my body couldn't move, and I was breathing heavily. And all I could feel was a deep, deep emotion about to let loose. I grabbed my jacket and stormed out.

All day long, I kept replaying that comment repeatedly in my head like a broken record. Maybe I overreacted, but it wasn't intentional. At this point, I had absolutely no control over my hormones.

That evening, in the shower I began crying. I remember Johnnie coming in and saying, "Babe, what's going on?"

"I dooooon't know!" I said sobbing.

Crying seemed to have been turned back on like an open faucet. I cried for just about everything, at any time. It could be a commercial of baby diapers, baby food, or anything that remotely had a baby involved. I cried watching the movie *Boss Baby*.

My life became a monotonous rollercoaster of—morning shot, agonizing pain, work, emotional breakdown, lunch, another emotional breakdown, pills, nap, dinner, more shots, another breakdown. And on those last few days, I would have to shove a fun horse-sized suppository either up my anus or vagina.

My body was going through some serious remodeling. While the routine was in effect, I just felt comfortable in loose fitting clothing just for the want of comfort, I wore loose-fitting sweatpants, baggy jeans, and dresses that could double as tents. Oh, and let's not overlook the grandma panties. Johnnie wasn't exactly doing cartwheels of excitement over my fashion choices, but he was a trooper. Despite my meltdowns, he wisely decided not to comment. Maybe he was afraid my hormones would launch a full-scale rebellion. Who knows, but in the grand scheme of things, comfort trumped my rage.

I focused on getting through the medications so we could finally get to Barbados. But that didn't mean we could just put our lives on hold. Johnnie and I still had social commitments. Two people we loved and adored were getting married and we had RSVP'd months before we even got the okay to start the medications.

And being the awesome planner I am, I had bought a dress for the wedding in advance (and before I started taking the medication). I bought this dress and was just in love—it was beautiful, fitted, and perfect. It was silky and hugged my body in all the right places. I was looking forward to wearing it. Plus, we needed a good day after all this. I needed to dance and celebrate, even though I wasn't drinking—that was ok.

On the day of the wedding, I did my hair and make-up. *I looked good!* Then, I went to get that beautiful dress out of the closet. I put it on, and the heavy feeling of my swollen body shocked me. I was extremely sensitive to the touch of the material on my skin. I took the dress off immediately thinking there was something inside it irritating me.

Finding nothing, I put the dress back on again and realized I couldn't move without some sort of sensitivity. I had to find a way to find comfort in this dress—I was determined to wear it. I decided to layer some gauze pads around my black and blue areas on my stomach to avoid irritation. I stuffed myself back into this dress, all at the same time screaming and sighing. The seams seemed strained, and I no longer felt stunning in this dress. I felt lumpy. I spun around in front of the mirror, watching bulge and bulge of fat sticking out. It had fit when I bought it, but now I felt like a stuffed penguin.

Still, I was trying to make it work. I had a thought—*a shawl!* That would be my saving grace. The shawl would hide the back bulges! As for the front, I would just use my hands to hide those. But I was determined to make this work!

I arrived at the church alone, as Johnnie was a groomsman and already there. As I began to waddle myself toward the front of the pews, I saw a group that looked familiar. They waved me over, and I smiled and began walking toward them. I felt the seam of the dress pulling a bit with each step, but I ignored it. I walked over and said hello and greeted some with hugs, handshakes, and kisses.

I realized my walk was more of a waddle and my uncomfortable feeling in my dress was a little annoying, but I still felt optimistic and happy for our friends who were about to tie the knot.

While moving around in my dress, an old friend of ours came up to me and hugged me tightly.

"Hello!" I said, leaning in for a hug.

SPLIT!

The back of my dress tore open, tearing from about my mid-back to my calves.

I breathed and cursed, "What the fuck?"

She looked at me in stunned silence, as I tried to play it off by saying, "Girl, what the fuck? It's been forever!"

Talk about inappropriate language in a church. But really—*What the Fuck?*

I tried to coolly back up to the nearest wall while trying to convince my friend she should go ahead and do the rounds. I kept smiling and waving to people, hoping that I didn't look as concerned or embarrassed as I felt. At the same time, I could feel a breeze on my back and ass cheek. The shawl I was wearing was only about half the size of a normal shawl so it couldn't cover my entire back. Not too long after the incident, Johnnie walked over and asked, "What are you doing here in the corner?"

"My fucking dress *ripped*!" I whispered.

"What!? Babe, let me see," He turned me around enough so that he could see and started laughing. "Babe, your entire ass is out!"

"I know!" I hissed back at him in full embarrassment.

Laughing, Johnnie took off his blazer and draped it on my shoulders. I was so anxious to walk out. I told Johnnie we had to go to the car. He laughed and walked right behind me as I walked out of the church.

My embarrassment morphed into anxiety and then into panic.

I couldn't just go home and change since we were so far away, so I whipped out my phone and started looking for a nearby store where I could buy something to wear.

No luck.

"Oh right, my gym bag is in the car!" I went to the trunk and looked for my gym bag. Even if I had to wear shorts and a shirt, I would still attend this wedding. I needed to be there to support our friends. That's when I discovered some dry-cleaning bags! There was a romper from H&M. *Score!* It was my saving grace. It was loose-fitting and comfy. And far better than shorts and a T-shirt.

I kept Johnnies jacket on my shoulders and ran back into the church to use the bathroom. As I took the dress off, I realized the six gauze pads I had put on were not there anymore, not stuck to the dress or on the bathroom floor.

I hurried up, threw the romper on, and began to high tail it out toward the ceremony that was about to start. I threw Johnnie his jacket and he ran in to meet the rest of the wedding party. As I walked out, I saw trails of gauze pads on the floor. *Omg, I thought I would die!* I walked and picked up the trail until I saw an elderly woman looking down in disgust. We made eye contact, and I gave her an agreeing disgusted look as well.

As I ran past her to sit down on one of the pews, I silently prayed that God would give me a baby and that all of this was happening for a good reason.

Chapter 16

Wanderlust and Paranoia

I was powering through the pain of the shots, anal suppositories, boatloads of pills, hormones firing up, swollen and black and blued stomach, weight gain, and embarrassing situations like the one in the church. Still, I was doing my best to stay positive. For the first time through this all, I felt empowered because I had been braving it all! *I was doing it!*

It was important to be brave and put on a brave face at this point because I had booked our plane tickets and a hotel for us to stay. This was it. I had about seven more days of shots and the clinic requested I go in for an ultrasound to see the size of my follicles. I hadn't stopped looking for a doctor while I was on my meds because I was aware that I would need another ultrasound. I found an Obstetrician who had just started. She was new, young, and easy to talk to. Plus, she was cool with my requests. She was happy for me and offered to help in any way possible. My back-and-forth feelings with U.S. doctors were wavering. *There were some good ones, after all.* She was able to do the ultrasound in no time.

Despite maintaining positivity and my new sense of empowerment, a persistent sense of loneliness had settled within me. Johnnie was incredible, but I yearned for a connection with someone who understood the intricate emotions and challenges I was navigating. In my quest for shared experiences, I reached out to close friends and family, hoping to find a kindred spirit who had walked a similar path. Unfortunately, my search proved fruitless, leaving me feeling even more isolated. Turning to the vast expanse of the internet and social media, I sought solace in online communities.

However, the few existing groups asked uncomfortably personal questions for entry, creating a barrier that I hesitated to breach. The loneliness that nestled in the pit of my stomach grew.

Johnnie used his power of persuasion, or more like his relentless argumentative points to help me. He told me repeatedly, "Stop trying to hide what's going on! We have amazing family and friends who want to support us. Let's lean on them." I want to say he beat me down, but honestly, I was so lonely that I relented. I loved talking to Johnnie, but I did need to turn to others. And once I was on board with talking to our friends about our struggles, let me tell you I was on board! I couldn't shut up about it. And it came with a lot of backlashes from some.

There were the not-so-appropriate jokes like, "Well, if you can't get your wife pregnant, let me give it a shot."

My response: *Nah, I think I will pass!* (while showing a face of disgust!)

There were God comments too: "If God wanted you to have a baby, he would have gotten you pregnant. You must have done something bad in your previous life and that's why you are currently suffering."

My response: *Well then, I am in a world of hurt; thanks for following in Jesus's way and reminding me of my shortcomings; I appreciate you!*

That response didn't land well, but something had to be said. I must admit that some of those statements did hurt as things got harder.

Let's not forget to add some of the stupider comments: "If you're trying to have a child, you can just have one of mine. Why do you want kids? They are expensive and a pain in the ass. You want your life to be miserable because I hate mine right now."

I would just simply smile and move on from that conversation. But besides all those unworthy, unfriendly statements, the majority were warm, comforting, and needed.

As the journey drew closer to the reality of heading to Barbados, a looming list of "what-ifs" clouded my thoughts. *What if this was some shady black-market operation aiming to harvest my kidneys? What if the clinic turned out to be a sketchy garage or backyard setup? What if I contracted a strange illness? What if, in the end, it was all a colossal mistake and wouldn't work anyway?* The weight of uncertainty mingled with my loneliness created a complex mix of emotions that clung to me, even as the anticipation of the journey intensified.

The days were approaching faster. "Consider this a holiday" was written on the catalog for BFC. The doctors told us the same thing. *Okay, I can do that!* So, I thought of my favorite holiday—Christmas. And my wish for this Christmas was an ... "All I want for Christmas is ... a baby," sung in my best Mariah impersonation.

Just the thought of the word "Barbados" and "Holiday" got me into optimal excitement. So now let's get ready and plan. I hate going anywhere without being prepared and this Baby Making Boss was going to be OVER-prepared for this trip!

Now first thing first: bags and bags of sunscreen and bug spray because I am a walking buffet for insects' mosquitoes especially. In fact, when I was planning the trip, Zika had just become rampant throughout the islands, and I felt such fear and concern for my safety.

Zika was of special concern for pregnant woman as it could be passed on to a fetus, causing brain defects. Mosquitoes find me in the winter, and I was not going to let Zika get a hold of me, so like any normal anticipatory anxiety-ridden person, I was on a hunt for the safest mosquito repellent out there. Open buffet, I would not be!

A folder full of past lab results. CHECK! Passports. CHECK! And, of course, I'll need my husband because babies don't just appear out of thin air (unless you're the Virgin Mary, in which case, carry on). CHECK!

Cute beach dresses and sandals. CHECK! Because typically, when you're trying to conceive, the most important thing is looking fabulous, right? This woman was ready for anything. But the most crucial element of all—an optimistic outlook, which I had been practicing for a while.

We were on an 8:00 a.m. JetBlue flight from LAX, with a two-hour layover at JFK, and then back on the flight to Barbados. In total, it was about a 10-hour travel time with one time change. As we walked into the LAX airport, JetBlue terminal, I completely froze. Butterflies fluttered endlessly in my stomach, along with continued horrible thoughts.

I watched Johnnie check our bags at the kiosk and scan our tickets and I could hear the "Law and Order" soundtrack in my head, *"Dum Dum."*

I yelled out, "Johnnie! Do you think they sanitize their tools? Seriously, what if this is some scam?"

"Babe, just stop. We are not buying into your fear and overthinking. Everything is going to be fine," he assured me.

"We don't know that!" Irrationality was setting in once again. "They could sedate me and steal one of my kidneys. I'll wake up in a bathtub of ice in some random hotel with a weird scar," my nervous babbling continued.

"I wouldn't let that happen to you," Johnnie said, trying desperately to comfort me.

Not one to be deterred easily, I continued, "What if they steal something different, like my eggs, OMG my eggs, and sell those on the black market?"

Worse and worse scenarios kept popping into my head.

"Babe, please relax. We did our research. This clinic is what we've been looking for," he reaffirmed.

As he watched me spiral into bad scenario after bad scenario, he suggested, "You need a drink, babe! You're killing me right now."

And I knew I was. I promised him I would tell my inner crazy to stay there and would have a glass of wine on the plane in hopes it would make me fall asleep.

Johnnie and I entertained ourselves on the flight by taking silly pictures and making each other laugh. We talked about putting all those pictures in a family photo album someday soon if things on the island went according to plan. We told ourselves we'd have fun on the island. We deserved to have fun on this trip, even though it was serious. Johnnie had been working crazy, stressful hours to pull off some major projects before we left. I'd been hopped up on hormones and juggling my work and life, too, trying hard to maintain my sanity and preserve our relationship.

My 'what-ifs' continued to overwhelm me as we approached the plane door. And as soon as we took off and the beverage service began, Johnnie ordered two glasses of wine. *Yeah, yeah! I know!* I knew I needed to change my diet and alcohol habits immediately. But I also needed something for my jitters.

"Positive thoughts, positive pregnancy," we repeated to ourselves and each other the whole flight.

This didn't stop my mind from racing, though. Neither of us had ever been to this country, despite seeing some beautiful pictures online. We didn't know what to expect. Was this a romantic, exciting movie that turned into an unexpected horror film, catching moviegoers off guard? I filled my eight-hour flight with stomach turns after doing all the due diligence on the doctors and clinic and thoughts about our financial situation, which was settled with my parents' help. I was on all the meds and injected my body so much that it looked like a used pin cushion. All areas were checked off. This is it! It's our time.

Nothing can go wrong. I was certain of this. *So, butterflies go away, and crazy thoughts leave me now. Let me have this.*

But that didn't happen.

Chapter 17

Bajan Heart

As the plane descended, my heart raced with excitement and a bucketload of nervousness. I couldn't believe we were there. I eagerly looked out the window, taking in the sights of swaying palm trees and vibrant, brightly colored homes. I immediately felt like you feel when you say, "Ahhhaaaa!"

This island was gorgeous! As we stepped onto the tarmac, we were greeted with a welcoming whiff of the salty sea air and delicious aromas of local cuisine. It was like heaven. We arrived in Barbados four days after Johnnies birthday. *What a birthday to remember!* We immediately saw that the island was just as beautiful as all the pictures we had seen on the internet.

As it's a small island, the baggage claim process was quick. We walked over to customs with my prefilled docs ready to hand over to the customs officer. "Are you bringing in anything?" the officer asked.

"Hmm, yes, I have some medication with me," I said.

I remember him giving me a weird look and instantly my stomach began swirling! Was this the start of the red flags of my concerns? *Why is he looking at me like that? Did I bring in illegal meds and it was all a set up?* I thought to myself. *I really need to stop watching these types of tv shows because they are messing with my mind.* I immediately volunteered my doctor's correspondence about needing these drugs from the clinic. The officer didn't budge and handed me back both mine and Johnnies' documents and told us to go ahead.

As we walked away from the officer and began the trek toward the exit, we followed the signs for taxis and car rentals. The car rental office was located right next to the terminal exit. We waited outside with our luggage until it was our turn. Although the airport was small, we had to endure a long wait before finally getting our rental car.

We were offered a small white vehicle. We loaded the trunk with our luggage and got on our way. I sat on the passenger side, with my seatbelt on, looking all around. While I sat there fidgeting, Johnnie was reviewing his map toward the hotel. Although it was hot, there was a warm breeze that blew through the open windows. We had been on a 10 plus hour flight and were tired of circulating air, so the fresh hot air felt amazing! The drive to the hotel was about 20 minutes. Along the way, we passed by impressive sights such as big, beautiful homes, golf courses, and countless palm trees. We also noticed outdoor vendors and familiar eateries, like good ol' KFC.

The atmosphere exuded a Caribbean charm! Each home boasted vibrant distinct colors. People strolled along the streets, children played energetically, and the city hummed with activity. Smiles were abundant, but it was hard for me to join in.

As we pulled up to the Radisson Hotel on the Platinum Coast. A yellow and blue hotel, serene from the outside. And I immediately fell in love with it, the color coordinated with the ocean right behind it!

I watched Johnnie struggling to lift my semi-overweight suitcases out of the car, and then felt a wave of panic wash over me again. "Alright," I yelled to Johnnie, trying to get him on the same page and join my nervousness, "We are here for a specific reason, so don't look too touristy. I don't want to be touristy!"

I stood in the middle of the driveway and looked around. I felt the eyes of both the bellhop and my husband on me like I was, in fact, just another crazy American tourist. *But I wasn't. I was here to get my baby!* Walking toward the reception desk, a beautiful, brown-skinned woman asked if we were there for vacation.

I looked around to see if she was speaking to us. She was. *Hmm I guess we really did look like tourists! Or did I look like a tourist? Or was it my full American accent?*

My nervousness turned into a full-blown comedic panic then.

"No! We are not here on vacation! We are here to do IVF at the Barbados Fertility Clinic. We want to have lots of babies, and I heard this is the place to get me pregnant," I shouted. *Why was I shouting at this woman? Ugh!*

"Oh, that is amazing!" she said with an interesting British accent with a Caribbean flare. "So many people come for that," immediately reassuring me without knowing it.

"Really?"

Now, she has my attention!

"Can you tell me more? Is it bad? Is it good? What's the deal?"

I leaned in to get all the dirt on the clinic from someone clearly 'in the know.'

As she stepped back from the insanely frantic American, she said, "The clinic, from what I hear, is wonderful! They are even in our magazines sometimes."

Okay, that felt good to hear.

As she continued to check us in, typing things on her computer, she told us about the restaurants in the hotel, our access to the pool, gym, and beach. Every morning the horse handlers bring their horses to the beach, so the horses can get a refreshing swim before the races. She then gave us our room key and wished us luck.

In all our calculations and dollar watching, I, of course, booked a basic room (needed to save wherever we could). But when we walked into the room, it was far from basic. It was huge with a patio and an ocean view. Did we get an upgrade? Did my obnoxious rant help me get this? Either way I was not going to complain. *Maybe I should try that at other hotels?*

As we were freshening up and looking forward to getting some dinner in the hotel, there was a knock on the door. The bellhop had a gift basket and two pillows in hand. We told him we didn't ask for extra pillows, but he said it was complimentary. I accepted those and the basket, not sure what it was or who it was from. I placed it on the table and looked in to see there was some candy, some fruit, a small pair of socks, and a small heating pad.

There was a card in there that read—*When you're done with your treatment, hopefully this will help you feel better.*

This was one of the most beautiful gestures I had ever gotten from a stranger. I wanted to thank the woman at the front desk, as she was the only person I had spoken with. When we went downstairs, I stopped to thank her, but was told she had just left and would be on vacation with her family. I spoke with the manager and expressed my gratitude for the basket I received and how appreciative I was. He mentioned that such a gesture is rare but the woman who checked us in is known for her compassion.

I wondered if she knew much about IVF. *Did she know the process? Had she tried IVF?* Either way, one thing was clear—she was another angel in disguise placed on my path to give me the signs I needed when I needed them most.

The universe knew I needed validation.

And it was proving it in spades.

Chapter 18

Embracing Nerves and Visual Aids

After dinner, I was able to somehow convince Johnnie we should do a drive by of the clinic so we wouldn't be late the following day and to help ease my fears.

"What if we get there and it's just not what we saw on the website?" I asked frantically.

"What if it's run down or isn't a clinic at all but some abandoned warehouse where shady people are going in and out at all hours of the day?"

Johnnie looked over at me, his hand on the steering wheel.

"If it looks weird, we don't have to go through with anything, but I really don't think it's an abandoned warehouse."

I was spiraling out of control.

"Babe! Breathe and relax. If we feel weird about it at all, we can hop on a plane and head home. Deal?"

"Deal," I responded, his calmness having some effect on me.

We drove around the clinic three times, and I memorized all the eateries and retailers next to it. It looked more like a house than a warehouse!

The next day, we had an early morning appointment. I woke up, and my nerves were already shot. I felt my stomach tying and untying into knots. I tried my best to ignore them and focused on getting ready.

I put on a very cute and flattering summer dress, with sandals, and did not use any makeup. The humidity was seeping through the windows of the hotel room, and it would just melt off my face. I put my hair in a cute ponytail. This is it! We were on our way .... *finally*.

As we got closer to the clinic, my anxiety only intensified. *Who knew it could get worse?* I couldn't stop staring at the right turn indicator on our last turn, watching it tick by as if it were mocking me. A moment later the structure came into sight, and it revealed its presence.

My stomach churned, and I felt like I was going to vomit. The only pleasant feeling was the smell of the ocean breeze coming in through the open windows. Johnnie continued to talk to me, but I heard only the faint sound of his voice, like he was whispering. And when he reached out and caressed my hand, it sent a sensation through me, bringing me back to Earth. As we parked Johnnie looked over at me.

"Are we doing this?" he asked, trying to decipher my non-usual quietness.

"We're doing this!" I looked over at Johnnie with more confidence than I truly felt.

"If it doesn't work out, there's a pub across the street," Johnnie said with a wink. *Of course, he would have found the pub!*

I gave him the annoyed look I'd given him a thousand times, but I couldn't help but crack a smile. "Okay, okay, we'll go there even if it *does* work out," he said. I fought a smile and stepped out of the car.

My heart raced as we walked up to the large white building—a tall gate enclosing it like a fortress. Its walls were pristine, off white, giving the impression of a mansion.

The sign on top of the walkway read, "Seaston House." Palm trees sprouted up around a well-manicured emerald lawn.

A small, wide staircase guided us up to the clinic doors. I pushed the buzzer and told the voice on the other end we had arrived. The voices in my head went silent for once, thankfully. I had no thoughts of being scared or even nervous. I was just completely silenced, taking in every detail. My body shook a little as I walked toward the staircase. My emotions were so raw and intense, I felt as if my heart was going to burst out of my chest. I couldn't help but wonder what the appointment would reveal and what it would mean for our future.

We heard the click of the lock lifting and pushed the door open. This was it—the moment of truth.

"We are here," I said.

"Positive thoughts, positive pregnancy," Johnnie said out loud, reassuring me.

I watched his lips mouth those four special words that we found ourselves saying to each other often over the past few months, and I summoned my body and lips to join in.

"Positive thoughts, positive pregnancy."

I put one foot through the doorway as the door opened and I just stopped. I froze. My heart raced but the rest of me felt paralyzed. I was right in the doorframe. Johnnie was behind me and couldn't get in.

"Babe, you've got to move. The door is closing on my back and crushing me," he said.

He pushed me forward a little and I stumbled in. Looking clumsy, and stepping into the room, my surroundings unfolded before me like a scene from a familiar drama. The walls, in soft hues, enclosed a space resembling the archetypal waiting room: a row of plush couches, pamphlets scattered on the coffee table, and the soothing hum of a water fountain in the corner. A mix of large, luxurious windows let in light that bathed the place in magic.

Behind the commanding front desk, a trio of women engaged in a ballet of paperwork. Upon my entrance, they collectively looked up, their smiles genuine (and *with* steady eye contact—*CHECK!*), and a harmonious chorus of greetings filled the air. The contrast was striking—a tangible departure from the sterile ambiance and people of the other offices I had visited over the past several years.

Amid absorbing this newfound warmth, the room suddenly echoed with the sweet sound of my name. Could that be for me? We just got here! (*No long wait—CHECK!*) My name sliced through the air, sending a ripple of awareness down my spine. I could feel it— I was entering a transition into a fresh chapter of my journey.

As I glanced around, my name resounded once more, this time in a voice filled with warmth. "Mrs. Mandy," the words emerged from behind the desk from one of the receptionists there. A petite figure emerged, her head bobbing up and down as she rushed around the counter with an infectious energy, creating an immediate connection between us.

It was Cyrilene, the head receptionists I had been speaking with on the phone and emailing. She was wearing a white skirt and floral top with arms out for an embrace. My body was in shock. I stood there watching her in slow motion, coming toward me. I have never seen so much excitement in a doctor's office, especially as it related to me. My heart skipped a beat as I turned to face her more directly. She spoke in a sweet voice and immediately wrapped me in her arms.

"We are so happy you are here," she said excitedly.

In that moment, a tidal wave of emotion crashed over me. The burdens of stress, anxiety, and uncertainty slipped away, replaced by the peace I found in the comfort of her hug. Tears welled up and streamed down my face as I leaned into her shoulder, allowing my entire body to collapse into the haven of her welcoming arms.

She then extended her embrace to Johnnie, pulling him into that same type of beautiful, comforting hug. In that shared moment, we felt a connection that transcended words, a connection that spoke volumes about the power of compassion. With her gentle touch lingering on our shoulders, she guided us slowly to the waiting room.

Not long after, I received the request to go into the doctor's office. I soon saw that our face-to-face meeting with Dr. Jones would mirror the warmth of our prior phone conversation. As the first person I had connected with before my arrival, she greeted me with friendly familiarity. Our discussion unfolded around the purpose of my visit—egg harvesting.

With a gentle demeanor, she showed us diagrams and visual aids to illustrate the intricate journey that lay ahead. Sensing the weight of the information, she paused and candidly asked, "Do you understand what I'm saying?"

I just stared at her.

"No, you don't," she smiled warmly.

I must have looked bewildered, because she responded with a warm smile, acknowledging the emotional and overwhelming nature of the subject matter.

We talked about the entire process, from soup to nuts.

She described the follicle-stimulating hormone I took to tell my body to produce more eggs because the more eggs I produced, the higher my chances of success. (By this time, my ovaries should have been decorated with clusters of tiny follicles.) Then she talked to us about the egg retrieval. She explained that I would be sedated under general anaesthesia and that I wouldn't feel anything while the eggs were being retrieved, but that afterward, I may be in discomfort.

She then explained the process of a guided needle attached to a catheter through the vagina and one by one, would draw the eggs out using light suction. *That's it! No stitches. No scars.* All while the eggs are being removed, Johnnie would provide a fresh sperm sample.

The sperm would be put through a spin cycle to find the healthiest swimmers (who hopefully swim in the right direction). They will then label the test tubes with my name and unique identification number, which the embryologist will collect. After the egg retrieval and the needle removal, she would examine my vaginal wall and ovaries once more.

She continued, "Once your eggs have been collected, we will provide another medication to prep the uterus lining for the embryos that will be transferred back into you. You will be in the recovery room with your hubby when you open your eyes."

We then talked about genetic testing and its process. This is an optional but highly recommended component of fertility treatment, especially for individuals or couples with a history of genetic disorders or recurrent pregnancy loss. What we were interested in was PGS, which is Pre-Implantation Genetic Screening. This screening is done on the embryos for chromosomal abnormalities, ensuring that only embryos with the correct number of chromosomes are selected for transfer.

Our conversation expanded to include the blastocyst stage, and the subsequent transfer, concluding with the nerve-wracking Two-Week Wait (TWW). Throughout this detailed journey, the doctor demonstrated patience and kindness. She took her time. She was patient with me and didn't rush me out of her office.

It was the next step that led to more concern.

Chapter 19

Nature's Nest to Science's Cradle

After that great first date with the doctor, we were escorted to another office where we finally got to meet face to face with the woman I called my email BFF, Dionne. She was our IVF Case Coordinator. Her office was a bit smaller than the doctor's office and filled with files and small picture frames scattered along her desk and on the windowsill. She was the person emailing me my list of meds, my schedule, my time frame and recommendations on where to stay. Every email from her felt warm and concerned, and we felt the same way in her space.

While in her office, Johnnie did most of the speaking, as I did a lot of head nodding and smiling, still taking it all in. A few minutes of jokes were passed around during our meeting. *Of course—Johnnie was in the room!* The process felt comfortable. I felt at ease with the clinic itself, with the staff, and with all the information they provided, including answering our countless questions. And by "we," I mean Johnnie's questions because I was still abnormally quiet. He seemed different once we touched down on this tropical paradise. I wasn't sure if it was the smell of the Caribbean breeze that made him super relaxed or the idea of trying pubs on an island, but whatever it was, I loved it! I needed him to be at peace and have his senses on so he could lead the conversation when I needed him to. Unfortunately, for me, it was difficult to relax.

"What can't we do while we're here on the island?" Johnnie asked.

"What do you mean?" Dionne responded back.

"What can't she do? Can she go in the water?"

"Enjoy the island and each other. You can go in the water. I would recommend don't go horseback riding and avoid diving too close to the procedure. Enjoy your time; this is a beautiful island! We also have our local weekly event where our vendors come out, set up stalls and outdoor grills and cook some of our traditional Bajan style foods and the highlights are the fish that is either fried or grilled. The community gathers and socializes with music along the beachside. It is something to check out!" Dionne responded.

Ok, so you want us to enjoy ourselves and relax all while trying not to think about what is about to happen in the next few days. Easier said than done.

But before we could possibly go and relax, I had to do my first ultrasound in their office. It was important to check the size of the follicles since I had completed the first round of medication. This would help see the exact day for egg retrieval, or if I needed more time on the meds.

A nurse led us into the exam room, where I changed into a gown for the ultrasound. Johnnie meandered around the doctor's office, looking for some kind of trouble to get into, as usual.

"Babe," he blurted. "You still seem nervous."

"I am."

"Hmm, I have an idea."

I wasn't paying him any attention as I was undressing and just seemed to be stuck still on my own fears, but when I turned around, I saw that he was sitting in the exam chair. Yup—there was my husband—shifting his body around to get comfortable, with his feet in the stirrups, spreading his legs like he was the one about to get examined. He then went into a full conversation about what the doctor said and how eggs grow. As I settled in on the cold chair with my gown clinging to my skin. I found myself engulfed in what he was saying not only mentally, but also emotionally.

"I don't know what you're always complaining about! This seems fine" as began to shift his body around on the exam table.

Just then, there was a knock on the door and the sonographer walked in. She looked at him, walked back out, closed it, and started bawling in laughter on the other side. Right then, two other nurses walked by and opened the door to see what all the commotion was about. They looked in and noticed Johnnie, who appropriately gave them a thumbs up and a big smile.

The sonographer walked back in and said, "You want an exam? Because I'll give you one!"

We all had a good laugh, and that's when I felt another nudge of ease.

As Dionne walked us out of the clinic she said. "There's so much to see! Go have some fun! I will email you about the follow up after we review your ultrasound."

"Be stress-free!" someone else yelled.

That word again, but with 'free' at the end. Amid attempting to relax, we decided to head to the beach for lunch.

Not coincidentally, right in front of us was the pub Johnnie had his eyes on the night before and this morning. They had a good lunch menu, and outdoor seating facing the ocean, so it was win-win for us both.

We laughed and joked, trying to keep our spirits up, but the documents that they had provided us with during the visit kept creeping back into my mind. They weren't difficult to read but did have us considering more questions we hadn't thought about before. The first page talked about embryo freezing storage and costs. *What do we do with them? Should we continue storage year after year? Should we donate them for research or offer them to some couple in need? Any couple? What if we divorced? Why would we get divorced? Who gets the embryos? Will these be fair decisions, or are they based on emotions now?* There were a lot of very heavy thoughts and decisions to make that day.

After lunch, we decided to take a walk on the beach. I would always experience a sense of healing once my feet touched the water, and that day was no different. I needed this more now than ever before.

We walked around for hours, sat on the beach, and watched the sunset. As we were heading back to the hotel, we stumbled upon a little tiki bar that was playing live music. We grabbed two seats at the bar, feeling the soft breeze on our skin and listened to a local artist perform. It felt so calming.

After about 15 minutes there, a couple sat next to us. We smiled in acknowledgment and continued to talk to each other. It seemed, though, that the couple wanted to join in our blissful moment. "Why did you come to Barbados?" the very petite blonde woman asked.

"Just a trip!" I responded back.

She began to tell us they were from Texas. Her husband, who was standing behind her a tall, broad man wearing sunglasses (after the sunset). He leaned in and said, "We are here on a work trip, and she is always asking to go away, I figured this would quiet her up."

"Do you have kids?" the woman asked.

"We're working on it," I replied.

Feeling a deep stare, waiting for more, I caved.

"We are going to try our first round of IVF here," I blurted. I couldn't help myself!

"We did IVF, not here, and it worked for us. We have twins," the woman responded.

Her obnoxious pushiness is what I needed that night, even if it came with her arrogant husband! She was excited to share with me all the funny things her twins do to make her laugh and how they were precious gifts through the process of IVF. She began to share how much she struggled and how emotional she was when it didn't work the first time. Her husband showed little excitement or sympathy about the struggles she had.

He said, "If a woman was going to have a baby, she should go through the fertility challenges alone."

He went on to express to two strangers that in this process, he couldn't be a part of it because he had to work, and she was too emotional for his taste. I was so angry at him … and so sad for her. After a few minutes of his negative statements, she slowly turned her stool, having her back to me the rest of the evening. I felt terrible, but I had no words to express other than that her husband was a real asshole.

As we walked back towards the hotel that night, we watched the waves dance gently on the sand and the moonlights reflection. I couldn't help but feel overwhelmed with emotion. Johnnie has always been my reliable rock and never on this journey did he ever disregard my emotions as this stranger did to his partner. In that same moment we noticed hundreds of baby leatherback turtles popping out of the sand and were racing to start their new lives. Their eyes were on the prize, of immediately getting to the water, using the moonlight as a guided light. For some it came with dodging a few swooping birds, seagulls, crabs, and other animals looking to snatch them up. While the babies were trying to defend themselves, hotel staff, and guests ran out to do some defense as well and provide guidance for the turtle's safety, using magazines, cups and plates to deter the predators away. I began to tear up, as it was the most beautiful thing I had ever witnessed. Johnnie and I stood there watching the last of the hatchlings rush to the ocean. What we saw was the emergence of new life, with an entire team rallying together to ensure its survival

I hoped for a similar outcome for us.

Chapter 20

Strength, Sperm, Superovulation

During the extra two days of medications, Johnnie and I continued to enjoy the island as much as possible. We also had not one, but two unexpected visitors. First, my dad, who came to Barbados to lend his support. And then our friend, James, who had been by our sides for this entire process, listening to all our concerns, fears, and my obnoxious theories surprised us with a visit. He could hear it in our voices we were scared.

Over the years, James went above and beyond to be there for us. His unwavering support gave us strength even when we felt like giving up. We had even asked James to marry us, and he had done so with the joy and sincerity that only a genuine friend could muster. He understood the depth of our love for each other and the journey that lay ahead of us. He lent an ear, spiritual guidance, and even asked us some tough questions.

On day three it was planned we would return to the clinic for extraction. We both woke up feeling tired. I wasn't the only one who couldn't sleep that night. To gear up our energy Johnnie played music and we began to bustle around the room getting ready. I tried on three dresses, as if my attire would wow the crap out of my eggs. I looked at myself in the mirror and spun around. My eyes said—*Yup, you look good!* My emotions said—*Yup, you're a hot mess right now.*

To distract myself I began organizing my prepped bag, packed in it was my gifted warm and cozy socks from my mom. There is a widely held principle in Chinese medicine that a "cold" uterus can cause infertility. It is believed warm feet equal a warm uterus. Now, logic was still somewhere on the periphery of my brain, and I knew that studies show that if your core temperature stays stable, and that is where the uterus is.

So, if your feet are cold, it wouldn't really change. However, when you go down the rabbit hole named 'IVF,' you will gladly follow all myths, legends, and superstitions for the best possible outcome. So, wearing socks wouldn't guarantee a pregnancy, but it would keep me warm anyway!

Also, in my bag ready with sunscreen, mosquito repellent, and all the signed documents. *Seriously, was I going in for a procedure or to lay out on the beach?* It didn't matter. I even checked my makeup and looked over at Johnnie to say, "Hey, are your players ready to?"

He posed with hands on his hips and said, "As ready as they ever could be. These Irishman are all set!"

I turned to him and his lower genital area and said, "Team, get it together, we need you on in this!"

And out the door we went.

We arrived at the clinic at seven in the morning, as requested with an empty stomach. My nerves were a wreck, and there was nothing I could do at that point. Both Johnnie and I sat in the waiting room holding hands until our names were called. We gave each other a long embrace, and a kiss.

"Don't worry he will be the first person you will see when your eyes open up" the nurse said.

Now, it is time to settle into a gown in a cold room … again. Time for the doctor to show her extraordinary skills. She would use a small vacuum tube device—an actual medical instrument (not some hoover vacuum from the closet) to suck my eggs out (I am sure she used a much better medical term but that's what I heard). Then begin to extract eggs that were of the appropriate size (each clinic has its own criteria for determining the appropriate size, although 16 mm seemed to be average). While I was under, Johnnie would be taking care of his part.

Later that evening Johnnie shared his experience with me. He walked me through how he was led to a private room at the clinic to manually stimulate himself until his efforts were, you know, fruitful. They provided him with a sterile collection cup to fill with ejaculated sperm. He later described it as a cold, sterile room, having a brown leather reclining couch and some abstract paintings on the wall. He was offered an old and presumably 'used a few hundred times' remote control to watch some sultry caressing on a small television in hopes of promoting a healthy, energetic, and solid specimen.

Just as I talked about earlier, "stress" plays a huge role in not just women but in men as well in the family planning journey. Your partner wants to be able to provide the A-team of sperm, the Michael Phelps of swimming, if you will. And this simple act that boys have been performing very successfully (ask any mom who had to wash a boy's bed sheets) since the age of twelve isn't as easy during these times.

At first, Johnnie struggled to watch the old school television that was in the room—the stimulating videos(porn) they provided, in his description, was "ancient." He said he then turned to the magazines on the stand next to him, catalogs of women in 1980s Europe. Some of the pages were stuck together. *Ewww!* If you knew my husband at all, you would know that he is a super germaphobe, not the Howie Mandel status, but close. So, this room was unbelievably uncomfortable for him. It was hard for him to get hard, literally, and physically. He decided to turn to old faithful, pulled out his phone, and found his go-to videos.

Finally, as he described it, he had some 'good momentum' going when he heard a sound that threw him off. As he looked around, he saw two men on the roof, washing the obscure windows. They were laughing and talking loudly.

"Fuck!" he cried out. "I need to get this done!"

"C'mon guys, can't you see I'm trying to beat my personal best here?" he said more to himself than to the guys outside, who had no idea what they were interrupting with their mindless banter.

Finally, he emerged victorious and sprinted over to the nurse's desk with his swimmers in hand.

Not long after I opened my eyes to see Johnnie sitting next to me. It felt like I had gone eleven rounds with a heavyweight boxer. My stomach was so sore I could barely move without wanting to keel over and cry. And cry, I did!

Thankfully, the nurse must have heard my pitiful sobs because she came running over with an entire arsenal of pain relief items to make me feel better. She had some pain meds to take the edge off, a cold pack to soothe my aching tummy, and some gentle caressing on my back to let me know everything would be okay.

As I struggled to gather my scattered belongings, feeling weak and tired after the procedure, a warm and comforting presence suddenly greeted me—my embryologist, a petite woman with a gentle voice and a lot of energy appeared. I couldn't help but notice her bright smile, sparkling eyes, as she showed happiness to see us. I stood there anticipating some good news.

With a soft voice, she explained the next step. Her words were clear and concise; she spoke with empathy, understanding the vulnerability I was experiencing.

She explained that my eggs were in the embryology lab, where the team would then locate, count, and place them in nourishing media that mimics the environment of my fallopian tubes. They were able to retrieve thirty-three eggs. *Holy shit!* I knew immediately that was a positive sign for the success rate. The more eggs you have, the higher the chance of a successful pregnancy. I was elated inside. Feeling very proud of myself at that moment.

So, suck it, you dick head doctor who said I was too old.

Next steps are to wait. And with no other options that's what we did.

Chapter 21

Anesthesia, Animals, and Acts of Kindness

Still feeling woozy, Johnnie carefully led me to the car and back to the room. I slept for hours. Although it was light sedation, my body takes anaesthesia like a blow—even children's Benadryl can put me under for two days!

While I slept, Johnnie did some work on the patio and met with James and my dad for a drink and to provide them with an update. I woke the first time to see him bringing me lunch. *So sweet!* Then, I was back asleep. When I woke again, there was dinner ready for me on a table by the bed.

The following day our support team were heading back home. After breakfast, we said our goodbyes and thanked them for supporting us. Johnnie and I were so grateful that we had such an amazing circle of family and friends that stood by our side.

I was able to stand up the next day but was still in some abdominal pain. I was sore and swollen. Waiting around in our charming hotel room with a view was nice, but all I did was just stare at the phone, waiting for an update from the clinic.

We waited. And waited. And waited some more.

"Babe, I don't know if I can take this anymore," Johnnie finally said.

"Oh, thank God, I can't either," I replied, relieved.

"Let's take a drive around the island," he said.

"Let's go check it out!"

The thought process was that we would give the clinic the time it needed, and they would reach us on my cell phone when they were ready. I had a fully charged phone, along with a charger.

The journey was meant to be a quick 40-minute drive, but our navigation app had other plans. Instead of smooth highways, it took us on a wild adventure down every bumpy dirt road in sight.

As we wound our way through the twists and turns, we were greeted by a scene straight out of a nature documentary—one where monkeys darted across the road freely and disappeared into the lush greenery. It was our own little jungle safari! The wildlife wasn't the only thing that caught our eye. The architecture was equally amazing. From sturdy stone houses to charming chattel homes, each building seemed to whisper stories of the island's rich history. And speaking of whispers, the air was alive with the chirps and calls of exotic birds. By the time we reached our destination, our spirits were as high as the island's palm trees.

Eventually we made it to the top of the beautiful North Cove Mountain. There was a panoramic view of the tropical landscape stretched in front of us that was breathtaking. It was the perfect spot to pause, which was exactly

We noticed a little restaurant along the edge and decided it would be a great place for a snack. As we sat down, I could feel my mouth watering, smelling amazing aromas from the kitchen. Apparently, all the wobbling around the car helped me work up a serious appetite. While we waited for the waitress to arrive at our table, I pulled out my phone to check the time.

Shit. Missed call. Ohh, four missed calls. Was it the clinic?

I had not heard my phone ring on the drive. *Shit! We didn't have service!* I tried to listen to the voicemail. It was the clinic, but I couldn't understand the message the nurse left. The service was shot in this area and all I could gather was every other word.

In a panic, I looked around to see that we were the only ones in the restaurant. I was too impatient to wait for the server, who was in the kitchen, so I jumped up and rushed over to the kitchen. I told her I had an urgent call I needed to make and asked if I could use her phone. When I finally was able to speak with someone, the team had all left for lunch. In a panic I yelled.

"Johnnie, we have to leave right now."

Luckily, the food came seconds afterward. We scarfed it down, paid with a nice tip, and rushed back to the car, shaken ovaries and all. I could not miss the clinic's next call. After finally showing signal on my phone, I called the clinic again. The assistant asked if she could have the nurse call the hotel room as soon as she was back.

"Yes, call the hotel," I said. "We won't leave the room; we will never leave the room!" I nervously chuckled.

Flustered, Johnnie tried high sped it back to the hotel. After about an hour long wait, we received a call from the embryologist everyday with an update for the next five days. I journaled every update and phone call.

Day Zero: Egg Retrieval & Fertilization.

33 eggs single and ready to mingle! It's time to mix my eggs with Johnnie's posse of swimmers. Johnnies' sperm were provided and ready.

Day One: Fertilization Check–About 14-16 hours after ICSI, an embryologist checks all eggs to confirm fertilization.

And we have fertilization! We have cells!

Day Two: Embryos divide.

We were down to 31 eggs. The other two hadn't properly fertilized or divided.

Day Three (aka Cleavage Stage): Embryo Grading and Potential Transfer. They grade embryos based on their number of cells and a grade of 1 through 4. The number of cells refers to the number of cells present in the embryo when observed under a microscope. A healthy "day three" embryo will typically contain between 6 and 10 cells. Several studies confirm that an embryo with 6-10 cells is more likely to grow into a viable blastocyst than an embryo with fewer cells.

By day 3 of fertilization, we dropped to 15 viable eggs.

Day Four: Cleavage to Blastocyst Transformation. Embryos are transitioning from cleavage to blastocyst stage.

Day Five (aka Blastocyst Stage): Blastocyst Grading and Transfer or Freezing. If embryos are carried out on Day 5, they will check them again.

Of those 15 eggs, 8 of them are ready to go out and be genetically screened. The genetic screening results would take at least a week to return.

Days Six and Seven: If an embryo hasn't reached the blastocyst stage by day five, it is typically monitored. Embryos that have developed into blastocysts can either be transferred or frozen. Embryos that have not progressed to the blastocyst stage are not considered viable and are usually discarded at this point.

Once we were told it was time to send out for the genetic testing in Chicago, we decided this was the time to head back home and await the results. As I began thinking about making flight arrangements a heavy and unsettling feeling washed over me. The reality of returning to our everyday lives, devoid of the temporary escape we experienced started to sink in. We would no longer be on "vacation" instead we would be left waiting anxiously for answers that could potentially be a positive or negative.

I tried to tweak our flight details online, thinking it would be a breeze. Turns out it was not. When I finally got through to an airline representative about our flight change. I was informed there was some serious extra charges for changing the flight. *There goes my pre-planned out budget.*

I then started to ramble again. "We came to this island for fertility treatments, they said I got some good eggs, so our next step is to go home and wait for the rest of the results."

Abruptly, the woman said, "Can I put you on hold?"

"Sure," I replied.

I waited, pacing around a little as the hold music played in the background.

"Okay, this is what I did for you because you just made me cry," she said.

"What?" responded back.

"I know what it feels like to want to have a baby," she said, her voice cracking.

"So, I changed your flight to tomorrow morning for free and gave you some credit for your next flight. I had to put you on hold because you made me cry!"

What just happened? I apologized to her for making her cry and caught myself crying too. Johnnie walked out of the bathroom and saw my tears.

"Who are you talking to?" he whispered.

"I'm talking to the lady at JetBlue," I said while crying.

Johnnie looked back at me, confused. He sat down with a cup of coffee in hand and just stared, likely wondering if I had completely lost my mind again.

I had not expected my story to resonate. I had not expected anything at all.

The kindness didn't end there. The hotel comped our dinner from the night before to wish us good luck. It was a strange feeling to realize how many people, who we would probably never interact with again, were rooting for us.

Feeling blessed in our hearts, it was time for us to head home.

Chapter 22

The Weight of Choices

I thought the flight to Barbados was bad, with all my emotions traveling with us nerves, anxiety, and a whirlwind of fear. But now, not only did those feelings decide to join us on the flight back, but they were joined by some agonizing physical pain the repercussions of retrieving thirty-three eggs from my tender body. My poor stomach was protesting, swelling up to the size of a grapefruit. I stood in front of the bathroom airport mirror and took multiple pictures of myself wondering if this was a sneak peek into what pregnancy might look like on me.

The 10-hour flight was absolutely agonizing. I requested tea and two blankets, but nothing worked. I sat next to a woman who kept looking over at me, wanting to know why I looked the way I did. As I held my stomach and tried to find a comfortable position. During a moment of comfort, she was able to find her opening to ask me if I had gone overseas for a tummy tuck and if it was a botched job. Prior to cabin pressure, I could talk to anyone who asked about my condition, but this time I was in so much pain, I just looked at her and started laughing.

I immediately turned to Johnnie. "Please switch seats with me. I just can't with the woman next to me."

He promptly got up and switched seats, put his earbuds in and instantly became the wall between us for my sanity. As we landed, all I could think about wanting was to be in my bed in my PJs.

Oh, to be home again!

The two weeks crawled by as if time were standing still. I tried my best to stay occupied. And then finally on one rainy day, I received a call from the clinic. I was told that with my eight embryos that were tested only three were viably healthy. In order of quality, we had the following: #1 46XX, #2 46XX, and #3 46XY, which meant two females and one male. The sun came up after that call.

My family! Our family!

I could see it. I could imagine my two girls and my boy. Johnnie would be outside playing catch with our son, and I would be hugging and playing dress up with our two beautiful daughters. It was the happiest thought I had. I felt elated. I cried for days, but this time, they were happy tears! After days of being a blubbering mess, we came up for air and we decided that we would share our results with our immediate family.

And they were all thrilled!

The next step was to reach out to the clinic and prepare us for a return visit. And this time I was ready! So ready, that I became anxious.

We didn't wait long—it was about eight weeks from when we were last there. If it were up to me, I would have left immediately, but with work and Thanksgiving right around the corner, we opted to freeze the eggs until we could get back. But before heading back, I had to prepare my uterine lining to embrace my baby. I continued with my vitamins and resumed going to the gym.

The challenging part of waiting was waiting during the holidays. There was always a sense of sadness during this these times for us. The thought of knowing I didn't have a little one in my arms yet for Christmas was sad, but I did have a present waiting. And that made me feel so happy inside. During this time, instead of attending holiday parties, I read books about being pregnant.

I looked at cribs, strollers, and baby bottles. I was in the rabbit hole. There were times I would stroll into baby clothing stores and when a salesperson would ask how old my little one was. I would smile and walk away.

What could I say? That I am the crazy lunatic woman shopping with no baby? At least, no baby *yet!*

After a lot of back and forth with Johnnie about our availability with work, and money. We decided that late January would be the perfect time for the transfer. We couldn't wait any longer! I couldn't wait! I wanted so badly for the holidays to hurry up and end.

Our plan would be to be back in Barbados on January 25, 2017, for the implantation of my freezer babies! I had this date stamped all over my notes and walls. This would mark the memory of something amazing.

Knowing that I wouldn't have to be sedated this time, and we could go for just a few days to do the transfer and head back home and do the Two Week Wait (TWW) felt better. During the past few months, we enthusiastically shared our experiences about Barbados with our friends John, Steph, Jimmy and Nandini. Our experience captivated them so much that it sparked the idea of a group trip. For both Johnnie and I, we welcomed the idea. Feeling it would be great to divert our minds and soul. Having their support by our side felt like a continuation of the support we received during the extraction.

I was not as emotionally stressed as the previous time. I must admit—I was managing it all very well. I was back in charge of those crazy emotions! No emotional outbursts. Zero fears settling in. I was ready! I knew this was going to happen! I was confident! I had mentally and emotionally prepared myself. Let's go!

Another 10-hour flight coming from Los Angeles, we almost felt used to it. Everything was working in our favor as we landed early, customs was a breeze. This time we decided no car rental was necessary since our planned stay with our friends meant either walking everywhere or cab.

We arrived at our Airbnb, weary but eager, dropping our bags quickly before heading straight to our first appointment at the clinic. Stepping through those familiar doors, it felt as though no time had passed at all. Warm embraces enveloped us again, with genuine smiles as comforting as ever. The staff greeted us with their usual warmth, yet there was a difference in the air.

In that moment, my heart swelled with an overwhelming sense of joy. I stood in the presence of possibilities. The mere thought of these embryos, each carrying the potential to fulfill my deepest longing for a child, filled me with an indescribable warmth. The joy of holding a precious baby in my arms, or perhaps even the blessing of multiples. For days prior to the visit, Johnnie and I talked about how many eggs we would want to implant, but we wanted to hear from the experts about the best way possible. We had three embryos—two female and one male.

This time, Dr. Jones was notably absent from the scene. While I tried to mask my disappointment, I had to remind myself to keep an open mind. I tried to find solace in the thought that the rest of the team had proven themselves to be exceptional. I attempted to push aside any lingering doubts, reminding myself that my past experiences with male doctors shouldn't cloud my judgment.

We were then introduced to Dr. Shay to discuss the next steps for our embryo transfer and our options for the greatest chances of success. Based on my lab records, my response to the meds, and my having 33 eggs retrieved, everything was looking up. It all looked like there may not be any reasons things would not work out the way we anticipated. *Great! Exactly what I wanted to hear!* We knew there was a three-day thaw time that needed to occur, so we had to decide in one day what we wanted to do.

His recommendation was to implant two of the best eggs, increasing our chances of successful implantation, which is when the fertilized embryo attaches itself to the lining of the uterus.

This was when I learned the word 'sticks,' referring to the embryo attaching to uterus and continue its development into a baby.

We asked about our options of implanting one verses two and about the possibilities of success. Johnnie was interested in having a boy and based on the three we had, he asked, "If we implant two, which ones would they be?"

The doctor stated it would be better to implant the top two which would be the male and the top female. Johnnie chimed back in with concern, "What if we implant both females first?"

He explained that he felt like the last on the list of embryos didn't show as high a quality for possibility. And that for a greater chance of success, it would be better to implant the top two which included the male.

I stood there and just tried to absorb everything he was trying to explain. All while listening to Johnnie ask question after question. The doctor reminded us of his recommendation for two but reaffirmed that it was our choice.

We walked out of the office still feeling positive, but also different and conflicted. This was too heavy—to swallow. I felt so conflicted. I didn't know what the right decision would be.

My thoughts were once again all over the place—*If we implanted two of the three, I'd only have one more shot at getting pregnant if neither of the two eggs stuck. Could we risk that? On the flip side, was I ready for twins if that were to happen?*

On the drive back to the Airbnb, all I could think of were two numbers—one and two. All while Johnnie kept trying to make sense of how to get the possibility of a son. *What if? What if we only do one and it doesn't work? What if we do two and it doesn't work? What if? What if we implant the male and female and only the female sticks?* Do we want a higher possibility or was being too careful hurting or helping our possibilities?

My mind constantly raced to the worst outcomes possible. *Well, I wasn't as in control as my peaceful flight wanted me to believe.*

By the time we got back from the clinic our friends had landed and settled into the apartment. Everyone was in their bathing suits, ready to have a fun time, and I immediately regretted my decision of saying it was ok for them to be there. *What the fuck was I thinking? This wasn't a vacation!* When they saw our faces and my red, puffy eyes, they knew something was up. They'd been anxiously waiting to hear what our next steps would be, ready, armed with questions and excitement.

I immediately felt like there was lot of noise even though the room was silent. I looked over at Johnnie to let him know that I couldn't handle answering any questions right now. I abruptly walked away from the group and into our bedroom, shutting the door to give myself some space to calm down. The bed offered no answers, leaving me to sit on the edge, staring at the ocean and playing different scenarios in my head. The weight of this decision felt immense; it could change our lives, and this felt like we were playing roulette.

Moments later I heard a knock on the door, thinking it was Johnnie, but it was the group. They were all standing in the doorway, their expressions full of empathy. Their faces said it all—*We can't make this decision for you, but we support you.* It was clear Johnnie told them about our options. Both Steph and Nandini walked into the room and hugged me.

"I don't think I have ever had such a heavy decision in my life," I told them.

Luckily, the group was about positivity, happiness, and family. Each one of them saw having a child as a blessing and knew what Johnnie and I were going through was important. Later that day, they collectively decided it would be good to get us out of the room to do something fun. They booked a private boat to get us out onto the ocean, offering that the water would provide a healing and a spiritual connection.

Both Johnnie and I always felt the water did something for us, and maybe they were right. And we should trust in its magic and its serenity.

I was agonizing over every decision now—even one as simple as whether to go on a boat or not. By that point, it seemed like any decision I needed to make was just too overwhelming. I was complicating everything. Finally, I agreed to go. I figured, why not? The answers could be found in the gorgeous blues of the Atlantic.

Little did I know it would.

Chapter 23

Perspectives Collide

Once I finally agreed to go, everyone excitedly grabbed towels, sunscreen and packed all the essentials. I splashed water on my face to reduce the puffiness. We all got our beach essentials and off we were. We all loaded into a small white minivan, reggae music playing and air conditioning pumping.

I had a horrible bubbling feeling in my stomach that I couldn't shake. Johnnie assumed I must be hungry and passed me a small bag of granola hoping it would ease my hunger. As I dazed into a void—the sound of the group chatting blurred into the background. Then, I heard the word "twins"—the word associated with the number 'two' I had been thinking about all day when I wasn't thinking about 'one.'—this snapped me back to reality.

"If I could have had twins, I would have done it," Nandini said.

"I had my children one year apart. Twins would have been so much easier! It would have been great if they started walking at the same time," Steph replied.

"Please, you were losing your shit when our little ones were small," her husband, John, noted.

"Of course, I was! They were one year apart. I did not get any sleep! You could sleep through a hurricane" as the banter between them went on.

"I don't know what I would do now if we didn't have children," interjected Nandini.

"I really wish you guys the best," said Jimmy.

As the conversation unfolded, I found myself in a surreal daze. Even regular social interaction felt like navigating unchartered waters. I couldn't figure out how to engage, and that weighed on me. Fortunately, I didn't have to worry about it too much longer because the van glided to a halt. We reached the boat dock, and unexpectedly, it got quiet. I sensed the collective concern with their glances and subtle inquiries hanging in the air as we began to get out of the van.

The weather didn't mirror my conflicting emotions—warm, with a gentle breeze whispering through the stillness, and sunshine casting a soft glow on the surroundings. Nature seemed to dance in contrast to the turbulence within me, creating a paradox—happy/sad; peace/stress; warm/cold. As we approached the vessel, a 65-foot white catamaran sailboat, the boat captain, a kind man with a British accent, extended a warm welcome. His steady handshake conveyed an immediate sense of reassurance. He went over the rules of the boat, the mapped-out plan, and the package we had bought (well actually, what the group chose as I was in my voided state). I really had no idea what the plan was, beside it being a full day out on the ocean, with a light lunch and drinks.

As we began to move around the boat, I headed right to the front of the vessel to see what was ahead. I took in the salty air and the incredible view. Johnnie hung out with the group for a bit and then walked over and sat with me. I know he was conflicted about being with our friends, while supporting me. He was doing the best he could. As we sailed, the captain proposed snorkeling.

The group eagerly agreed. I watched as the captain anchored down; I was mesmerized at the flow of the anchor for that moment. Thinking how an anchor has so much stability to hold such a big boat and I was feeling so unstable in this moment. All while I was dazed the group began to move around the boat with excitement grabbing snorkels, and fins. One by one, jumping off the boat and splashing around in the crystal-clear water. I stayed on the boat, watching from afar as I tried to keep it all together. Johnnie tried to bring me into the fun. But I politely declined.

"Get in the water. It'll calm you down!" Johnnie said, as he was getting prepared to jump in.

"No, it's ok!"

Johnnie immediately jumped in and made a loud splash, then screamed, "Babe, come in! The water is amazing."

"No!" I yelled back.

As I watched them all swim in one area, looking up at me on the boat. They all began to shout out, "Come in! It's so great!"

"Come on!"

"Come on, girl!"

"Jump! Jump!" Johnnie screamed.

I began to get frustrated with everything. It rattled me. The clinic's request for our decision made me anxious and panicked to the point of shaking and breaking out in a nervous sweat. Here I was playing out scenarios for best outcome, and then hearing Johnnie's incessant screams (not to mention everyone else's). *Enough!* After feeling pressured and annoyed I randomly grabbed a lifejacket, clenched my jaw, and set out to prove something as I unsophicatedly pencil dived into the bright blue.

The warm water enveloped me swiftly and I quickly descended about 8-10 feet underwater. Despite my better instincts, I opened my eyes expected the salt water to sting, but it didn't. While my life jacket attempted to bring me back to the surface, the ocean seemed intent on gliding me further down. Suddenly I sensed something unusual around me.

A silhouette began approaching, and gradually becoming visible through my blurred vision.

It felt eerily reminiscent as it came closer, I was startled at first, but then felt strangely calm. This shape I saw in the past, with delicate features of bright brown eyes and hair. The whole experience seemed almost dreamlike, fuzzy, and veiled.

In that moment I felt a harsh tug and was forcefully ascended. And like ripping a band aid off, I broke through the surface of the water, frantic and trying to find my bearings. As I looked around, I locked eyes with Johnnie.

"How far down did you go? We were looking for you!" Johnnie observed.

The group began swimming my way, "You were under water for a bit" Someone shouted.

How was that possible? Did I grab a child's life jacket? How long was I down there? I wondered if I had knocked myself unconscious. I looked up at the boat and saw the captain.

He looked over at me and asked, "Are you okay" he said panickily.

"I'm fine," I screamed back to him.

With a flotation device secured to my body, I descended further into the abyss, both literally and metaphorically. It was a leap of faith, a hope in the darkness as I jumped.

Although I wasn't exactly sure what happened or what I felt, there was a calming sensation. The calmness was what I needed to stop overthinking and trying to be in control.

Johnnie stayed and swam by my side in the water. He looked over at me with concern and curiosity. I turned to him and said, "I think I know what we need to do."

While on the boat drying off, I told Johnnie I felt a sense of relief. The weight was lifted off my shoulders. The tears had dried, and I stopped agonizing. Unlike me who needed some sort of universe intervention to give me the clarity to decide, Johnnie only needed a moment to bounce his feelings off his friends and his heart.

And so, we both agreed and finally felt confident and comfortable with transferring two embryos! I rummaged through my bag, pulled my phone out and called the clinic. I looked over at Johnnie while I was on hold, holding my breath at the same time. I then took a deep breath and told the embryologist our plan. She seemed excited about our decision, and so were we.

That night as we watched the sunset along the horizon, we were offered a sense of peace. Peace of mind and soul. I finally let me self be okay to enjoy what was in front of us. We were fully energized and excited to go the next step of this journey. I slept amazingly that night and the night after that.

Unfortunately, it didn't last long.

Chapter 24

Transfer and Salty Fries

The time on the island was fun with our friends with amazing memories. As we came closer to the date of transfer, I began to feel anxious, and restless. My imagination ran wild, conjuring up different scenarios and possibilities.

The night before the transfer, sleep finally claimed me, but it was a restless one. Anxiety weighed heavily on my chest, making each breath a struggle. I woke up early with anticipation coursing through my veins. For this part it is necessary to drink multiple glasses of water to help ensure the success of the procedure. My bladder had to be full, pressing against my abdomen, altering the angle of my uterus. It was a necessary discomfort.

It was an early Saturday morning and as we stepped into the clinic. There were warm greetings as usual. Although I wanted to reciprocate the genuine good morning wishes to everyone, my emotions had a tight grip on my voice, rendering me almost speechless. A few minutes of waiting in the waiting room, all I could think about was the need to urinate. Finally, the receptionist led us down a corridor, the soft sound of footsteps echoing in the clinic's early-morning quiet.

Both Johnnie and I were led toward the surgical room. I was instructed to undress from the waist down, cover myself with a warm sheet and lie down on the exam table. Every movement was deliberate. Johnnie put on the full-body paper scrubs that were given to him, and gloves, his excitement clear.

"It feels like I'm going to do the surgery," he said with a grin. He seemed extremely excited about this decision. He had a smile on his face, already exuding proud dad feelings. I, on the other hand, was obviously uneasy.

I was shaking, and as the medical staff moved around and asked me questions, it was hard for me to comprehend anything. The transfer was soon to begin, a delicate procedure guided by skilled hands and hopeful hearts. I held onto the belief that this moment, this act of placing the right number of embryos in its rightful place, would bring us closer to fulfilling our dreams. I threw my legs up in the stirrups and waited for the doctor. At that moment, silence enveloped the room. Clasping hands, our fingers interlocked, we knew this was it.

The room was dim and cold, giving me goosebumps. There was a large screen in front of us, capturing our attention and setting the stage for what was to come. Across from me was a glass window, and all I could see was a head with a blue medical hair cover popping up and down in a flurry of activity. To my left stood two nurses, on my right, was Johnnie and my doctor. I glanced around, my eyes darting nervously, trying to find comfort.

This room held the most important people who could make the impossible possible. Just moments later the procedure began, and the doctor inserted a soft catheter into my cervix under the guidance of ultrasound. We were then to place our attention on the screen in front of us and followed its lead. Soon, it was time for the embryologist to do her magic, with the assistance of the accuracy of science. The embryologist's precision in loading the embryo into a catheter and transferring it in a tube through my vagina and cervix. As the tube carried the embryo, it forged a connection between the microscopic world and our eager eyes. Through a microphone, the embryologist's voice resonated, and began narrating the journey of our precious cargo.

The atmosphere in the room was tense in its extreme focus. As the nurses and doctors attentively watched the embryos journey on the screen before us. I found myself staring intently, but all I saw was a black screen with small circles of white marble all around.

What I was hoping to witness was something dramatic, something that would allow me to say, "Yes, I see my baby!" The doctor began explaining each delicate step on the screen and looked at me for confirmation. I nodded yes, even though I did not know what the hell I was looking at. The images and descriptions he provided seemed abstract and elusive to me.

"Oh, there it goes, there is one and now two," the doctor exclaimed, his voice filled with anticipation.

I continued to nod along, trying to feign comprehension, but I still saw nothing. *What is wrong with me?* I couldn't help but think. He then pointed directly at the smallest speck on the black-and-white screen. The confusion and frustration surged inside me, and tears welled up in my eyes as I glanced over at Johnnie.

"You don't see it?" Johnnie asked, his voice filled with concern.

I shook my head, feeling a mixture of disappointment and fear. I wanted to see what was visible to everyone else. I needed to see my babies! Johnnie looked at me, touched my forehead with one hand, and tried to point at the smallest specks of hope on that screen.

"It's okay," he whispered, trying to console me.

My doctor's gaze fell upon me, accompanied by a subtle nod of understanding. "Don't worry! We know what we are seeing. It's normal. I will print it out and show you exactly where it is."

I looked at him with tears on my face and nodded ok.

As I laid there, I could see and hear the staff moving around as the procedure on their end was complete, but not on my end. I had to lie in the stirrups for another fifteen minutes with a full bladder.

Within minutes, the doctor handed me a perfectly cut picture of my babies and drew a circle of them to make it visible for me. I focused hard on what was inside that precious red circle. Our perfect babies were in front of me. It was clear the doctors had been down this road before, likely with countless other confused and emotionally charged women. The minutes crept by, and I was preoccupied up until the need to use the bathroom.

However, a daunting fear crept in. *Would I accidentally expel the carefully implanted embryos if I peed?* The thought paralyzed me with anxiety. Yes, I thought I was in danger of peeing out my babies!

With those thoughts, albeit irrational thoughts, I hesitated to use the bathroom. The nurse asked me if I was ready to go and I said no, even though I really wanted to. I thought possibly if I could hold it long enough, I could guarantee these babies sticking. But moments later, I felt that I would explode. I was assisted to the restroom and then as I sat there, I couldn't go again. I scared myself! Then there was a light knock on the door, politely reassuring me it was safe. As soon as I heard those words, it was like a dam broke and the pressure in my stomach was relieved.

As we prepared to leave the clinic, there seemed to be an electric excitement in the air, everyone was excited and hopeful. The recommendation was to go home, relax, and avoid heavy lifting. Oh, and no hot tubs! Sexy time was possible after a few days. I listened intently as I was not going to ruin this.

After we left, I glanced back at the clinic that gave us so much hope, while simultaneously causing so much anxiety—it was an ironic contradiction. After a moment, we stopped for a magazine cover kiss and then headed to the car, leaving the clinic in our rearview. In following most advice offered we had to include having McDonald's fries after the transfer! *Hey! Any excuse, right?*

Since there was no McDonald's nearby, we opted for large French fries with salt from the neighbouring cafe. It felt like the most delicious thing ever. Was it the taste of salt or the feeling of excitement? Whichever it was, it was amazing.

Now onto the waiting …. *Ahh, the waiting game … once again.*

Chapter 25

Another "F" Word

The morning after the transfer, we were back on a flight to Los Angeles. Our friends had left the day before, not before wishing us luck and prayers.

Once our fourteen-day wait began, it was agonizing. Each day was filled with anxiety and uncertainty for both of us. Through it all, Johnnie's unwavering support steadied me—keeping me afloat when I thought I would drown in worry. With each passing day, our connection seemed to deepen to an entirely new level. We already had a strong bond, but now it was cemented through our shared vulnerability and faith in our family's future.

To distract me, Johnnie took me on various outings. We went dancing. We went out to nice dinners. We went for walks in the park. We also went to concerts. We embarked on little day trips, all designed to keep my mind away from the constant planning and testing. Although these activities didn't fully divert my attention, I deeply appreciated his thoughtful gestures to keep me occupied. Every twinge or hint of tenderness became an opportunity for hope—a backache, breast tenderness, or even a sudden wave of nausea would immediately trigger the thought that I might be pregnant. I clung to any possibility, grasping at straws in my longing for a positive result.

Then finally the thirteenth day was here, and I could no longer contain my enthusiasm. I dashed around the house, clutching a brand-new pregnancy test.

"Babe, I'm going to test now!" I declared, unable to contain my eagerness.

"Babe, it's only one more day!" Johnnie calmly responded, reminding me that the doctor had said to wait *at least* two weeks before testing.

"I have to do it now! I can't wait until tomorrow," I pleaded, urgency filling each word.

Johnnie patiently waited for me to exhaust my energy and then said firmly, "No, we will wait one more day!"

In an instant, I deflated like a balloon. I bounced from one corner of the room to another, unable to sit still as my excitement morphed into disappointment. I looked at Johnnie, sat down with a frown, grabbed my blanket, threw it over my head, and sulked like a punished teenager.

That night, I tossed and turned, consumed by anticipation. On my nightstand, I kept the pregnancy test and a glass of water ready for the moment. As soon as 5:00 a.m. rang on my alarm, I jumped out of bed. Turning to wake Johnnie, who was already awake. I kissed him quickly on the cheek and hurried to the bathroom.

Excitedly, I held the pregnancy test in my hand—urine streaming onto the white plastic stick. A moment later, Johnnie walked in and sat quietly beside me on the edge of the tub. He set his phone timer for six minutes. And in those silent and tense moments, we both awaited the outcome, silently praying for our next chapter of three (or four) to begin. When the alarm finally sounded, I rushed to the sink where I had placed the test, my heart pounding out of my chest.

I looked down at the counter and immediately saw the words "Not Pregnant" on the stick's window. My heart stopped. I trembled, and tears welled up in my eyes. Johnnie paused for a moment, and then immediately urged me to take another test. After an hour of waiting, we checked again, only to find the same devastating result.

My heart shattered into a million pieces. I crumbled on the bathroom floor, tears streaming down my face. I could hear Johnnie asking questions, but I lacked the strength to respond. He hurried into the bathroom and instructed me to call the clinic. With tear-filled eyes, I looked at him and whispered, "I can't." He took my phone and made the call himself and left a message for our Case Coordinator Dionne to call us back asap.

We sat there anxiously waiting for a call back. And when it rang, Johnnie quickly answered. It was Dionne on the other end, who suggested we check my HCG levels and see if those sneaky pregnancy test might have played a little trick on us. Apparently, those tests aren't always accurate. *Who knew?*

Suddenly, a glimmer of hope sparked. This emotional rollercoaster was not ready to let me off the hook. I thought—*Of course, there is a chance the test is incorrect! What was I thinking?* Battling my fear and sadness, I located the nearest clinic, dialed their number, and practically begged them for emergency blood work. Despite the usual appointment policy, someone finally sensed my desperation and allowed us to come in right away. *Hallelujah!*

We rushed to the hospital like maniacs. Surprisingly, on a Friday morning, there was no wait. They swiftly drew my blood. Now for another agonizing hour of waiting (but we were getting very use to it by then).

Johnnie suggested we grab some food instead of sitting in the parking lot like a pair of starving zombies. It was already eleven o'clock in the morning and we hadn't eaten, so we headed to a nearby restaurant. Johnnie ordered eggs over easy with toast while I couldn't eat a thing. I settled for a cup of tea, trying to distract myself by scrolling through social media.

As Johnnie's plate arrived, I burst into tears. *Yes, tears from eggs!* Johnnie looked down at his breakfast in confusion, dumbfounded by the situation.

"Why are you crying?" he asked, clearly taken aback by my emotional outburst.

Through my sobs, I blurted out, "Because why would you order eggs over easy?"

Every second felt like an eternity, waiting for that hour to pass. The weight of anticipation settled heavily upon me, as I urged (okay, yelled), "Johnnie, hurry up and eat!"

We pulled up to the hospital's parking lot again and I looked at Johnnie. My voice was trembling as I pleaded with him to retrieve the results. I just couldn't bring myself to move.

I waited in the car, which felt like I was being marooned on the loneliest planet. Anxiously, my hands automatically clasped together, I asked God to provide me with this family I wanted so desperately. I offered a compelling description that God wanted this as well, because why would he have allowed me to get this far. I tried to frame logic, science, and prayer to him showcasing why this was a great situation for all of us. Just as I looked up, I saw Johnnie making his way out of the hospital doors I tried to discern any hints from his body language. *Was that a buoyant stride, filled with joy? Or is that just how he walks?*

I strained my eyes but didn't see a piece of paper clutched in his hand. It was driving me crazy. He was finally coming closer to the car, and I mustered every ounce of strength to wave my hands in a frenzy, desperate for him to reveal the news. He looked me in the eye and asked, "Do you want the good news or the bad news?"

At that moment, I wanted nothing more than to strangle him. Of course, I wanted the good fucking news! But a flicker of doubt clouded my mind.

"I am not in the mood for jokes, Johnnie."

His gaze remained fixed on me as he uttered those words that shattered my heart, "The good news is the labs are done." And just like that, my heart plummeted to the ground.

"And the bad news is we are not pregnant," I mumbled, my voice barely audible.

He met my gaze with a look of profound regret and whispered, "I'm sorry, babe."

It was as if time stood still. I could almost feel my soul departing as I struggled to take a breath. The world around me lost its vibrancy, its colors, drowning in shades of black and grey. We sat in that parking lot holding each other.

Me visibly crying and Johnnie sniffling trying to hold it together for the both of us.

Chapter 26

Home Again

That grey existence, devoid of color and light, persisted for days. I isolated myself from the world in sorrow and extreme pain. I ignored phone calls and text messages from friends and family.

Johnnie tried his best to help me, but most of the time, he respected my silent plea for solitude. All I wanted was to hide beneath the covers in a darkened room, shielding myself from the harshness of reality. I barely ate, barely slept, and work became an alien concept. Happiness eluded me entirely.

The world taunted me with reminders of what I lacked. Women strolled by with baby in hand, and strollers attached with baby toys, bottles, diaper bags. Baby commercials filled the television screen all day long. There were happy families everywhere—a constant presence, amplifying my pain.

After about 4 days, I mustered the courage to rise, eat, and wander around our place. Johnnie's face lit up with a mixture of relief and joy as he witnessed this minor victory. Unfortunately, the break was brief. I received a phone call from Lynette my sister-in-law, and it shattered the fragile thread of hope I had. Her voice heavy with urgency, as she had to share some devastating news.

"Hi! How are you doing? I tried calling you a few times to check on you. I also tried Johnnie; he told me you weren't ready to talk. I get it! But I really need to talk to you about your mom," she said with a gentle voice.

"Hi," I said back, devoid of any emotion.

I didn't have it in me to answer her question about how I was feeling.

"What's going on with Mom?" I continued.

"Well, I have been calling her for the past few days and I either get her voicemail or she said she will call me back. Two days ago, I called her and said, 'Mom where have you been, I have been calling you. Are you alright?' She told me that she was good. But something didn't feel right with me. I told her I would be by her house the next day. The following morning, I showed up at her house and I asked her what was going on and why she had ignored my calls. I thought she was going to laugh it off, but she looked at me and started crying. I asked her what happened, and she said they found cancer in her other breast. She said she didn't want to burden anyone, and she knew you were hurting right now and dealing with your loss. I told her that you are strong, and that she is just as important. I told her I was going to tell you and that's why I have been calling you."

While I was listening to my Lynette speak, I began crying my heart sank as her words pierced through me like a thousand daggers. While I battled my sadness, my mother was now facing another harrowing battle—breast cancer. She had shielded this heart-wrenching truth from me, believing that my burdens were already too heavy to bear. I hung up the phone and screamed aloud. My heart felt so heavy.

I was so upset by the news, but at the same time so grateful to my Lynette for being the daughter my mom needed then. They had always been close, and I had never been more thankful for their bond.

Later that day, I had to find the energy to call my mom. She sounded hopeful and was more worried about me. I asked her the same questions as before. *What did they say? What stage are we in? When is the next appointment?* This time, I approached the situation with my mom and cancer better.

I fell into a deep sleep because of share exhaustion. I woke up the next morning already knowing what we had to do. I told Johnnie we needed to move.

"What? Move where?" he asked.

"Back to New York."

"Okay."

I could see he thought this was just one of my crazy thoughts I come up with regularly and didn't believe it was true.

"When were you thinking?" he asked.

"We have to sell everything and go back to my mom. Now! She needs me, and I need her," I explained.

Johnnie just looked at me, slapped his desk, and said, "Well, guess we are moving back to New York!"

Johnnie has always loved his home and he missed his family and friends just as much as I did. For a long time, he longed to go back, but with work and us settled in Los Angeles, it made sense for us to stay. There was no need to leave ... until now!

Later that week, I was hell bent on selling everything, taking pictures of furniture, and grabbing garbage bags to fill with donations. As I began to organize my desk, I noticed we had RSVP'd yes to a friend's baby shower. *What the fuck was I thinking?*

I looked at the invitation and then dropped it on Johnnie's desk "Oh shit, we have to go to this. It's this weekend."

I shouted from the kitchen, "We are *not* going!"

There was silence. Then I heard him walking toward the room. He looked me in the eye and said, "Babe, we said we would go. Let's go. It's co-ed and there will be lots of alcohol. It'll do you good to get out of the house."

That logic didn't resonate well with me, but he seemed excited to attend a baby shower. I knew it was to meet and hang with the guys, so I had to take that into consideration. It wasn't only me feeling sadness.

I debated going for three days. I wasn't drinking, so alcohol wasn't my deciding factor. But I do need to get out of the house. I rattled off a bunch of questions, in hopes that Johnnie would be able to answer them logically.

Question: "Will there be pregnant women there?"

Johnnie: "I'm sure there may be a couple. I don't know. I don't go to these types of things.

Answer in my head: *Of course, there will be, there always is!*

Question: "Will there be babies there?"

Johnnie: "I'm sure. Again, I don't usually go to baby showers. But Mark said there will be a lot of men there, so it won't be the typical baby shower. Some sort of Jack and Jill shit your crazy gender calls it," as he walked away laughing.

Answer in my head: Of course, there will be.

Question: "Will I be, ok?"

Johnnie: "I will be there with you. And we don't have to stay long. Get in, get out."

Answer in my head: *I'm not going. Hmmm I don't know about all of this.*

And on the last day, I caved.

And it was probably the worst decision I had ever made.

Chapter 27

Reflections on Expectations

Saying yes to this baby shower was like agreeing to navigate a maze of discomfort, grief, and flat-out excruciating pain. I mustered up the courage, showered, got my makeup on, got dressed, and practiced my smiles. I had to put that RBF away.

"If you don't want to go, we don't have to go," Johnnie said that morning.

"I want to be supportive," I said, still unsure.

I told myself repeatedly that I was happy for our friends, and I wanted to be part of that happiness. Just because I didn't have what they had didn't mean I couldn't celebrate with them. As we pulled up to the house, I noticed a lack of cars and people outside which put me at ease. Maybe I could do this after all. As the door swung open, it was as if I had stumbled into a twisted version of Alice in Wonderland. Balloons floated in the air, kids ran amok, and pregnant mamas seemed to multiply before my eyes.

It was like a punch in the face.

I went to turn on my heel and walk right back out the door, but our friend saw us.

"Mandy! Johnnie! It's so good to see you," he said, walking over to give us both a hug.

Fuck, we can't leave now.

Even as he released us from the group hug, I couldn't move. My feet suddenly felt like heavy cement blocks. My knees immediately locked, and I couldn't turn around to leave, or move even one inch closer to the party full of happy people.

I stood stuck still for what felt like a century until this older lady came up to me filled with energy, hugging me tightly and whisking me away to the food table.

"Come on, you need to eat!" she said, gently grabbing my arm and pulling me further in.

She expertly loaded a plate with her homemade pierogies, cabbage and noodles, some meat, and potatoes, as well as an array of salads. It all looked delicious. I followed her lead, grateful for something to distract me from looking up and around—even if it was food. As I caved and surveyed the room, I noticed Johnnie had joined the corner occupied by the other men, toasting, and talking. I took a deep breath, resigning myself to my fate, and wandered aimlessly, searching for a quiet spot. Then, like a beacon of hope, I spotted an empty table far away from the chatty pregnant moms. I thought—*Aha! This is my haven.* I settled down, thinking no one would notice me, and secretly hoped that this baby shower ordeal would soon be over.

Suddenly, a little boy ran over to me with a piece of cake in his hand and sat right next to me. He didn't say anything, he just sat there. My immediate thought was—*What the fuck? Why me? This is my space! Move! Why are you sitting here?* We each kept an eye on the other, not saying a word. I tried to muscle him with a look that said go find another place to sit, but it didn't work. Just as the silence settled, a woman with a baby joined our table, gracefully breastfeeding her little one. Our eyes met, and she gave me a knowing nod, signaling that she, too, sought solace in this quiet corner. And just like that, our table of four sat together in silence, finding comfort in each other's company.

A few moments later, a young woman showing a little pregnant bump sat on the last seat. We all acknowledged her, and then each retreated into our own solace. It was as if we all shared a longing to escape the surrounding chaos.

And all I wanted to do was to scream "get away from my table." But nothing came out of my mouth.

I didn't belong, I wanted to belong.

I focused on my plate, my head down, and prayed some kind of intervention would occur for us to leave. My prayers obviously didn't work. From the left side of the house came a *very* pregnant, boisterous, determined woman. I'll call her "Grewretch-in," waddling her way to our table. She was bold, with her loud voice echoing through the room, making it impossible to ignore her presence. Every eye in the vicinity turned toward her, including mine. She stood looming over our table, her body language exuding power.

She approached the young woman, her belly proudly protruding, and fired away, "How far along are you? Do you know if it's a girl or a boy? I hope it's a girl! I have three boys, and my life is a disaster. I can't have nice shit because they break everything."

I watched the young woman try to answer the questions fired at her, but Grewretchy decided she was taking too long to answer and quickly shifted her attention to the breastfeeding mom.

"Is this your first?" she probed; her scrutinizing gaze fixed upon the poor woman.

"When I had my second, he would just latch on and not let go. I had the worst feeling in my breasts. I told my husband he needed a vasectomy because we were done. I hate being pregnant. I can't see my feet. I have heartburn. All I want to do is drink. I should drink alcohol, and it will make this asshole inside of me come out sooner."

As the breastfeeding mom desperately searched for a moment to respond, I realized it was my turn in the line of fire. To evade her interrogative prowess, I lowered my head, repeating a silent mantra, "Don't look up, don't look up." But curiosity got the better of me and panic surged through me as her eyes locked onto mine, waiting eagerly ready to pounce.

Unfazed by my lack of an obvious baby bump, she questioned me with a mix of surprise and disbelief, "So what about you? How do you know the shower hosts?"

I had quickly mentioned I knew the father-to-be, explaining that my husband and I were friends with him.

"Are you pregnant?"

Yup! There it was.

Time seemed to stand still as the weight of her question hung in the air. At that moment, I sought solace in the eyes of the young boy devouring another cupcake. He shrugged his shoulders, dropped his napkin, and darted away, leaving me yearning to do the same. But there was no escaping this situation.

"We're working on it," I replied with a smile. "Well, when you do, you're going to be fucking miserable," she said.

I forced out a chuckle.

"No, I'm serious," she said. "I feel like shit all the time."

She just went on and on, oblivious to how insane she sounded to me. She had it so good, and she didn't even realize it. From where I was standing, with what I had just lost and what I wanted so desperately, I couldn't conceive what she possibly had to complain about.

She continued, "Well, you should wait. You need to enjoy your married life without children. I told my husband I wished we had never had them at all."

I looked around for something to save me from this ranting.

My body was still processing all the hormones. I visualized myself slapping the crap out dearest Grewretchy, and then yelling at her at the same time with every obscenity on the planet. But in real life, I didn't have the energy to do anything but plot an escape.

I hadn't realized that Johnnie was nearby and overheard the barrage of questions from the pushy mom to be. To me, he appeared like a superhero, grabbed my hand, and blurted out, "Are you ready?"

I looked at him in shock and enthusiastically replied, "Yes!"

With a quick nod and a smile to the ladies at the table, I said goodbye. In hindsight, I wish I had the power and words to tell her off. I am the same person who was ready to go to jail over a doctor telling me I was *old*. I just lacked the energy at the time.

As we walked toward the doorway to exit the house, not saying goodbye to anyone, we ran into another couple coming in.

"Hey you guys leaving, so early?" they asked.

I turned and looked at the woman with tears in my eyes, and it was as if my soul spoke to her.

She turned and said, "These fuckin pregnant bitches."

I burst into laughter—it was exactly what I needed at that moment. I explained to her that this whole situation had become too much for me, and all I wanted was to crawl back into my bed. She understood, gave me the tightest hug ever, kissed Johnnie on the cheek, and expressed her love for us both.

On our ride home, I couldn't hold back the tears any longer. I turned to Johnnie and began pouring my heart out telling him how hard this was for me. In between sobs, I uttered, "If we ever get pregnant…" Johnnie interrupted me, correcting, "*When* we get pregnant."

I repeated after him, "*When* we get pregnant, I will never complain about a single thing during pregnancy. I will love every single moment of it." I promised this to myself and to him.

This woman's questions, her emotions, and her words about her pregnancy might have stung a bit, but they served as a reminder to cherish the extraordinary journey we are on together.

Chapter 28

Confronting Shadows

What was meant to be a celebration of new life both for our friends and a return to normalcy for us, felt more like a harsh reality check. It was as though life had unexpectedly slapped me in the face, reminding me of the stark contrast between our own struggles and our surroundings.

I realize that in the grand scheme of things, we're all consumed by our own battles – whether it's navigating the complexities of relationships, the discomforts of pregnancy, the demands of parenthood, or the relentless grind of work and financial concerns. It's easy to become so absorbed in our own struggles that we forget to truly see and empathize with those around us, even strangers.

But what if, just for a moment, we were to pause amidst the chaos of our own lives and truly consider the struggles of others? What if we could recognize that the unhappiness we carry within us might be the smallest desire or need for someone else? Maybe, just maybe, in those pauses lies the potential for understanding, empathy, and a deeper sense of connection amidst the chaos of life. As I would have preferred that woman to have considered, and then I would not have wanted so badly to retreat into my shell.

I tried to dive into work and went through the motions of the normal day-to-day routine, all while continuing my packing for our move. Our dinners at home became quiet affairs. In the evenings, I would lie on the couch or bed, consumed by my own despair. Even our long walks lost their appeal. I stopped taking care of myself—neglecting my workouts and even my vitamins. I was losing myself in the depths of my own sorrow and grief.

During one of those evenings, as I lay in bed, I reluctantly checked my email. I noticed four emails from the clinic, all urging me to schedule an appointment for a call. I ignored them just like I did with other multiple requests from work, as well as personal emails.

One evening Johnnie was able to finally coax me out for dinner at one of our favorite restaurants. As I sat there quietly reviewing the menu, I could feel there was a something that he needed to say. I noticed he jumped from topic to topic without any real direction. Until finally, I began to get impatient and motioned him to say what he needed to say. It was clear he had been preparing a speech of some sort.

"Babe," he began, his voice filled with concern, "I know you're struggling with everything that has happened—the loss and now the worry for your mom. But this isn't you. You don't laugh. You don't smile anymore. I miss my wife, miss my girl. I'm willing to do whatever it takes, and I am really trying to help us, but you're not working, and we have bills to pay. You're not doing anything, and I really feel overwhelmed. Your focus is us moving, but all the work is on me. I will do as much as I can, but I need your help too. I am not trying to make you feel bad, but you should start talking to someone who knows how to help you."

I stood there and stared at him with anger and frustration. How dare he say I am not doing anything?

The suggestion of help initially filled me with uncertainty and doubt. *And what did he mean by help? Therapy?* In my mind, I reserved therapy for "crazy" people, and I didn't want to see myself as one of them! *Did Johnnie see me that way?*

As much as I boiled internally with his words, my body caved as if I secretly knew I wasn't doing my best. I knew I wasn't happy; I knew I was going downward. Tears fell down my face as he spoke to me. Words could not be formulated in my head to argue back, and so I just dazed into space while hearing his words.

At this point, he was the only person I didn't push away. He was the only person in my space. And he was the only person I would listen to.

As I stared in a daze at the menu, he asked, "Would you let me help you find a therapist?" A mere head nod was all that I could offer at that moment.

Days went by as I replayed his comment in my head over and over. What did it really mean? I wasn't sure I even knew or understood, but I had agreed to asking and finding help, so it was time for me to begin the process of looking for a therapist. I started again with the good old insurance. We had already spent $12,000.00 on the treatments and now we were fully tapped out financially, so there was no feasible way I could have afforded an out-of-pocket therapist.

In hindsight you would think that therapy would be included in this process of fertility treatment. It would have been so much easier. Having a therapist as part of my medical team would have provided invaluable support and guidance, making the journey less daunting. Just imagine someone with professional understanding there to provide you with coping strategies, tools for resilience, and a supportive ally to lean on during the highs and lows of the process. It would have been nice to have had this already set up instead of me having to go on another search.

So, here we go again!

I was able to find only two options, one man and one woman. Apparently, my insurance is shit because no one else wanted to accept this coverage. With my lack of options, I felt more drawn to the female therapist, believing that she would better understand my perspective and struggles. I needed someone who wouldn't judge me and would be better able to understand my pain or at least explain to me what my pains were and how to resolve them quickly, since I wasn't really in the presence for Johnnie.

It was a nerve-wracking experience from the start. I did not know what to expect when I walked into her office.

Imagine a charming office space that was once a cozy home, now repurposed for small business owners such as a therapist's office. It was a two-story structure that retained the nostalgic feel of a 1970's grandma's house.

The décor of fake flowers and floral patterns on every surface from the wallpaper to the couch you sit on. I couldn't help but think—*Is this the right place? Have I made the wrong decision, by choosing this woman? Will this person even understand me? Am I secretly concerned about her age?*

As I entered the office, I laid eyes on the therapist herself—an older white woman who looked nothing like her profile picture. Short blonde hair, slim figure—she seemed like someone who wouldn't relate to a word I had to say. I immediately judged her, thinking this was doomed before it even started. In my head I had one other option, but since this was already booked, I went along with it.

My therapist (let's call her "Lisa") asked me to take a seat, and the session began.

"Tell me why you're here," she asked.

I stumbled for words, unsure of where to begin. Looking at this older lady, frustration and anger bubbled inside me, and I blurted out, "My husband and I were trying to have a baby, and it didn't work."

I glared at her as if she were to blame for my struggles. I blamed the universe. I blamed the doctors. I blamed Johnnie. I blamed everyone. While I knew it was not the therapist's fault, I needed to blame someone.

The real blame was me. I blamed myself, my body, my mind. *I knew one day I was off by a few minutes of doing my shot. Maybe that did it? One day I had problems getting that suppository up. Was that it? I had to do a shot in a restaurant bathroom because I wanted to hang out with friends. Maybe that was it? Or maybe it was because I didn't see my babies on that monitor that day?*

My eyes squinted, ready to unleash all my pent-up emotions on her. And it all came pouring out (and I mean *all*). My voice quivering and tears streaming down my face as I revealed my mom had been diagnosed with breast cancer again.

"I feel lost, confused, and utterly hurt. I can't even find myself anymore."

As the tears streamed down my face, my anger transformed into a torrent of an emotional breakdown. I blubbered through my words, desperately asking her, "How do I fix all of this?"

She observed my state of crying and talking simultaneously. I even cracked some silly (albeit inappropriate, given my track record) jokes, attempting to lighten the heavy mood that I, myself, was creating. I don't know why I was trying to make her laugh—I suppose I was feeling uncomfortable in that vulnerable state.

She wasn't much of a talker, I felt like I was talking to a wall. I kept asking questions, hoping for some guidance, but she remained silent. As time passed, my impatience grew, and I began to doubt if she was the right therapist for me. How could we make progress if she wouldn't even engage in conversation or offer any direction? As my session was nearly over, I began to fidget and got anxious to just wanting to leave. Then finally she spoke and asked a very simple question. I should have been able to answer quickly, but this one was thought-provoking. Amidst all my personal turmoil, she asked, "How does Johnnie feel about this loss?"

It caught me off guard because, as connected as I thought we were, I had not even stopped to ask him how he felt. While I had been drowning in my sea of emotions, and he had been consoling me. I wasn't there for him. At that moment, I felt like the worst person in the world. It wasn't just happening to me—it was happening to us both. *Seriously, what the fuck is wrong with me?* And yes, I fully realized I was again focusing on me, but I was just so disappointed in myself ... on top of everything else.

The drive back home was silent—no music, just me and my thoughts (a good thing, as I was alone). The weight of my realization pressed down on me, and I replayed her last question over and over in my mind. *How does Johnnie feel about this? How could I have missed this? How could I have been so self-absorbed?*

A lightbulb flickering and it hit me! *I needed to do something, something that he will see that I am thinking of him.*

With determination in my heart and a rumbling stomach, I headed to his favorite deli and grabbed a lunch that was meticulously filled with all that he loves, making sure not to forget the extra pickles on the side.

Armed with the lunch bag and a surge of hope, I made my way home. As I walked into the apartment and approached his desk, I noticed the weariness in his eyes reflecting a deep-seated fatigue and lack of energy. He had been shouldering my burdens without me even realizing it.

"Johnnie," I said, trying to sound nonchalant as I extended the lunch bag toward him. "How about we take a break from work and enjoy this outside? It's such a gorgeous day!"

His eyes lit up with surprise, and a smile slowly spread across his face. He willingly left his desk behind, and together we went outside and sat at a picnic table in front of the building. As we settled down, surrounded by the soothing sounds of chirping birds and rustling leaves, I felt a pang of guilt. It was time to address the elephant in the room.

"Babe, I'm truly sorry," I said remorsefully. "I didn't ask you how you felt about this whole situation. I was so consumed with my own emotions that I failed to see your pain."

He looked at me, a mix of sadness and understanding in his eyes.

"It hurt me too," he confessed, his voice barely above a whisper. "I've had my fair share of tearful moments in the car, questioning what the future holds."

My heart shattered into a thousand tiny pieces. *How could I have missed his silent struggles?* At that moment, I realized the depth of his love and support, and I couldn't hold back the flood of apologies.

A glimmer of a smile appeared on his face, and he reached out to hold my hand. "I understand," he whispered. "While I didn't experience the physical discomfort of the medication or egg retrieval or transfer, I still had the same longing for a family. I prayed for a family, too. And I knew you would make an incredible mom. I still know that."

Tears welled up in my eyes as I looked at the man sitting beside me. At that moment, all the pain and heartache seemed insignificant compared to the love we shared. I squeezed his hand tightly and whispered, "And you would be an amazing dad."

And so, under the warm sun, filled with light laughter and tears, we found solace in each other's arms. The journey ahead might be uncertain, but together we were ready to face whatever life had in store—one lunch break at a time.

After that one question on day one of our session, I decided Lisa (my flower loving) therapist understood me more than I prejudged of her. Some days, therapy felt like a breath of fresh air. There were also days when it seemed like she had a desire to provoke me intentionally.

In one of our meetings, she posed another question that made me squirm uncomfortably in my seat. She asked if I had reached out to the clinic to discuss the next steps. I confessed I hadn't mustered the courage to make that call yet. The clinic had left me a few messages, but I simply wasn't ready to face the reality of the situation.

Curiosity sparkled in her eyes as she asked, "What do you think they will say to you?"

At that moment, I hesitated, trying to summon the courage to speak the truth. "I don't know," I muttered, averting my gaze. I feared they would deliver the crushing blow, the words that would shatter my dreams by saying.

"You should give up. There will be no children in your future."

That is where my mind had wandered over the past several weeks. I convinced myself that the clinic held the key to my fate, and their verdict would seal the deal. The irrational part of me believed they had a solemn duty to tell me it was all over, that my journey toward motherhood was a lost cause. And truth be told, I really didn't want to hear those words. So, I resorted to the age-old tactic of ignoring their messages, pushing the inevitable conversation further into the depths of my subconscious.

We also took some time to discuss my need for blame. It was tempting to point fingers at the fertility clinic. But without concrete evidence, I couldn't bring myself to cast that blame.

I researched and researched, immersing myself in the complexities of the IVF journey. I had multiple consultations with other fertility specialists delving into the intricacies of my own body. I researched the limited information and education on my endometriosis—a condition only one clinic had acknowledged as a potential factor. I meticulously studied every detail, from the nuances of reproductive science to the specifics of Johnnie's sperm. I was nowhere near medical school, but I felt like I was in it.

Despite my exhaustive efforts, I found no one to blame. Science, for all its advancements, couldn't offer a definitive answer. We expect it to hold all the solutions, but sometimes, it falls short. Was it my genetic makeup, was my body not ready, did I have any other underlying issues? Was it a twist of fate, or simply not in the cards for me to conceive?

Through introspection and guidance, I came to accept that I had done everything within my power. I had turned every stone, explored every avenue, and faced every truth. And in my heart and mind, I found solace in knowing that I had fulfilled my duty to myself.

My insurance only allowed 6 weeks of sessions, in which I used every bit of it. I was approaching my final sessions, not just constrained by insurances timeline but also coinciding with our planned moving back to New York. Timing had become crucial on multiple fronts.

As I said goodbye to those therapy sessions and confronted the uncertain future ahead, Lisa suggested finding solace through a ritual or symbolic gesture akin to a burial. Closure was essential, and the idea of honoring this journey resonated with me, yet I struggled with what exactly to do and how to do it. Months went by as I pondered over this, searching for the right way to mark this moment in our lives.

Chapter 29

Cycles of Hope

After the exhausting task of packing up our lives, maintaining constant communication with my mom to reassure her of my support, and diligently applying all the breathing techniques recommended by the therapist, both Johnnie and I found ourselves craving space. We needed distance from each other, and it felt like the right thing to do. So, when Johnnie mentioned he was going out with the guys, I thought it was a fantastic idea.

My plan was to indulge in a binge-watching session of whatever show caught my interest. After he left, I reached for a Chinese food menu, dialed for delivery, and snuggled up on the couch with my favorite cozy blanket. I was fully prepared for my Friday night alone. As I sat there, absentmindedly scrolling through options on the television screen, my phone suddenly interrupted the silence. Glancing at the caller ID, I noticed it was my brother Robin. Curiosity and concern for my mom pushed me to quickly answer the call. His concern was apparent in his voice as he greeted me and asked how I was doing.

"I am okay," I answered.

He immediately went on to talk about his family and how fortunate he and his wife, Lynette (my sister-in-law) is. He continued by saying that they had two beautiful daughters and, although they had decided not to have any more children, it didn't mean they couldn't conceive. His words left me puzzled. I couldn't figure out what he was trying to say.

A long pause hung in the air, and suddenly, Lynette spoke, her voice filled with determination. She expressed their willingness to carry a baby for us. At that moment, my eyes welled up with tears. The sheer magnitude of their gesture, and the thought process behind it completely overwhelmed me.

My voice quivered as I tried to respond, conveying my gratitude, and letting them know it was too much to ask. Yet, they both reassured me of their love and desire to help, urging me to consider it as a viable option for us.

After I hung up the phone, waves of emotions washed over me, and tears streamed down my face. In that vulnerable moment, I couldn't help but think about the possibility they had presented. I waited up for Johnnie to come home, but he had had a lot to drink, and although I really wanted to share what we were offered, it just didn't seem like the right time. I figured I would wait till he was sober in the morning.

The next morning, I woke up with the words on repeat in my mind, echoing the voices of my siblings who urged me not to give up. As I sat up to prepare my mind and body to start the day, my phone notification chimed with a reminder that I had several unread emails, which were from the clinic.

I decided to face my fears and open those dreaded emails from the clinic. I was expecting a big fat "no baby for you" message, but to my surprise, they were all emails of options staring back at me! *And guess what?* Much to my disbelief, I completely forgot that we had a frozen egg just chillin' in the freezer! *How on earth did that slip my mind?* I mean, seriously, amidst all the chaos in my head, I never even considered that as an option! It's like my brain played hide-and-seek with important information. Without hesitation, I dialed the clinic's number and scheduled an appointment to speak with the doctor.

A Monday morning phone call went as expected. My demeanor on the phone was very mild. I figured that because I didn't respond to any of the emails or phone calls, I would be getting a lecture or discussion on my response time, and I was not prepared to have a defensive answer or attitude.

So, to avoid any conflict I had a lot of *ahhhmms* and "I guess" response. At the other end of the call, it was more like, "I am so happy to hear from you! We tried to reach you a few times! Honey, are you ok?"

Our Case Coordinator Dionne, whom I had a great relationship with earlier, seemed genuinely concerned, and I got the sense she knew I just needed to hear about my next steps. She went right into what my options were. "You currently have one egg here in our facility. We can implant that one, and/or we can discuss going another round to see if we can get more viable eggs to increase your chances. What are your thoughts?"

And like a deer in headlights, I just froze. I didn't really think of the options prior to the call.

"I don't know what I want to do yet. Can I talk with my husband before we decide?"

"Yes, of course. We want you to make the right decision for both of you. Just remember, we are here."

"I will and thank you," I responded.

As I hung up, I was more in a daze than one would expect. The conversations were better than I thought, but it was back to my thoughts again. *What does all this mean? And do I want to go through this again? Can I manage the emotional side of it. How do I bring this up to Johnnie again?*

That evening we had a long, long talk about my mental health, my mom's future surgery for breast cancer, our move back to NY and our future. *Should we even add more to our plate? How much will this cost us again? Will my parents help? And last, are we both in agreement about doing this again?*

After a comical and chaotic week of ping-ponging ideas back and forth, we decided that with our plate already overflowing, why not add some more to it? Scheduling the implantation of the last embryo and maybe even doing another round.

Why not overwhelm ourselves with chaos and see where the cards lie.

Chapter 30

Triumphs Amidst Turbulence

The looming May return to New York held the promise of familiarity, but it was overshadowed by the impending storm of emotions tied to my mom's scheduled mastectomy in June. Her surgery took center stage. Living out of suitcases, Johnnie and I found ourselves taking refuge in my childhood bedroom, grappling with the challenges of starting anew.

June arrived quickly and the surgery was a success. My mom was back home within two days, and her healthcare team assessed a speedy recovery. It was important for her to follow the post-operative care instructions to promote healing and minimize complications. However, as her body embarked on the journey of healing, her mental state took an unexpected turn.

Both my mom and I were dealing with our mental health for entirely different reasons. I noticed she was displaying signs of depression, something I was familiar with. Summoning the courage to speak out, I interrupted her appointment with her doctor and expressed my concerns. The doctor's gaze shifted from her laptop to my mother, and with a heart full of empathy, she asked, "What's going on?"

The unspoken exchange between them unfolded, and my mother's defenses crumbled into tears. The weight of her emotional struggle spilled out as she confessed, "I just keep thinking, why me? Why did it happen to me again?"

Tears welled in my eyes as I witnessed her vulnerability. Both of us in one room thinking—*Why me?* And as much as I wanted to help my mom, I didn't have any answers. Her doctor was gentle in suggesting seeking the help of a therapist, offering a lifeline to navigate her emotions. I agreed to accompany her to the therapy sessions, determined to do whatever it took to help her find the strength to heal not only physically, but emotionally as well.

While continuing my healing process we decided it would be the right time to engage in crucial calls with the clinic, working on a concrete plan for our return to Barbados. Before proceeding we agreed to do a blood testing for Natural Killer cells (NK). Specifically, we opted for a Peripheral NK cell test, which involves a blood work analysis aimed at identifying the presence and activity level of the cells in your body. The reason for this test after a round of IVF is to gain insight into how the immune system, particularly NK cells, maybe impacting the success rate. With this information the doctor will have a targeted treatment plan. The decision was daunting but inevitable—we would undergo another round of treatment while simultaneously transferring the last remaining egg. As I approached my 41st birthday, the urgency to preserve any potential healthy eggs intensified.

Within six months, my mom started feeling better both emotionally and physically. I felt like a thousand pounds had been lifted off my shoulders, and so we decided this would be the right time to head back to Barbados.

As I geared up my body and sorted out my leftover meds before they expired, I found myself diving back into full preparation mode! *Again!* This trip, much like the previous, didn't involve a direct flight, and there was no waiting in terminals. This pleasant layover was made in Trinidad. The trip had a dual purpose. At 63, my father decided it was time to earn his college degree, marking a significant milestone for his life. It was a joyous occasion with my mom in remission, my dad graduating and us taking another shot at it (literally and figuratively). Being that BFC has a sister location there it felt like serendipity, coming to the same location where my father initially suggested we seek treatment.

The first few days in Trinidad I administered my own shots, and the process was still the same, sweating profusely, panting heavily and nervously shaking. But this time around, I had an audience to provide all the necessary and unnecessary commentary. I could hear the "ouch," "eek," and "that looks so painful" comments every time. Though annoying, it was funny. Not long after it seemed like everyone wanted to be part of the process.

My nieces would stand there holding my hands while my sister-in-law administered the needle into my stomach. Right after, my mom wanted to hold an ice pack on my tummy, and my dad was standing there tearing up and offering me tea. This was a full-on family ordeal, and much appreciated.

After the graduation and festivities, Johnnie and I went to the airport for a mere two-hour flight to Barbados—shortest flight we had since starting this process. As familiar as we were with this routine, I intern didn't want to repeat exactly everything, so my attitude and attire were completely different. I was in my sweatpants, a neck pillow on and an eye mask on my head. I no longer cared about what I was wearing. The last time we were there, I was hopped up on positive thinking and hope. And this time, my mindset was vacation mode, and vacation only. I was not going to not over think this process. *Was it the right way? I don't know!*

We arrived at the clinic the morning after our arrival to discuss the plan. The warm hug from the "comfort connoisseur" was just the same. Our meeting this time around was a bit different, as we had already been through the formalities, introductions, and education in the process. This office visit was more to discuss the plan for the next few days, checking the size of the follicles, right time for extraction and transfer. We decided after the implantation we would get back on a flight the next morning. There was no need to stay longer.

Three days on the island was just the break we needed. The day of the egg retrieval Johnnie didn't have to leave our hotel room to provide his semen sample. He opted to provide his semen that morning. The timeframe for providing semen for an egg retrieval can be a few days before, to the day of the actual procedure.

Early that morning, while I meandered around the room and prepping my bag Johnnie was in the other room handling his business. I eavesdropped on the door a few times to see if things were successful. It was very quiet, or those doors were super solid. Either way he was getting it done. As soon as he was done, we got on the road.

Back at the clinic for a 9am appointment. Now time to get ready, socks on, gown on, arms outstretched, legs lifted into position, I glanced to my left to see the reassuring figure of my anesthesiologist preparing to administer the sleep-inducing concoction.

After being out for who knows how long, I opened my eyes, and saw Johnnie sitting by my side as promised.

I had the same pain as before, but not as intense. And there was a reason why. As I was getting myself ready to get up and back to the hotel room, our bubbly and full of energy embryologists walked in. I listened to the enthusiastic report of my retrieval of 8 eggs. For her, it was a promising outcome, particularly given my age—I was 41 years old. However, for me, the contrast was stark and somewhat disheartening. Just two years earlier, at the age of 39, we had harvested a staggering 33 eggs.

The disparity between then and now begged the question: *Where did this leave me?* As I grappled with the reality of my diminishing egg count, I couldn't help but wonder about the implications for our fertility journey. Would this smaller yield of eggs be enough? Was our chance at success slipping away with each passing year? These were the uncertainties that gnawed at my mind. *Why wasn't the math not mathing. It's best I just rest my body and mind tonight as tomorrow is a big day, focus Mandy!*

The next morning, we were at the clinic once again. This time, I was refreshed from my sleep, with minimum dark circles under my eyes, feeling good and ready to do this process again. We decided to do a full round of acupuncture before and after the transfer. Acupuncture is often used as a complementary therapy to help promote relaxation and improve blood flow to the uterus, potentially enhancing the chances of successful implantation.

Some people report feeling more grounded and centered after acupuncture, while others may notice a decrease in physical tension or discomfort. I felt so relaxed and at ease this time. This was something I wish I had agreed to in my first round. *But you live and you learn.* Now time for the transfer of our third embryo.

I hopped up onto the bed feeling a bit anxious and the same butterflies came fluttering back again. I stood there and silently prayed. My eyes darted around, ensuring everyone was in the right place: Johnnie to my left, the nurse to my right, and the doctor in front. I glanced overhead to confirm the embryologist was there as well. After completing my internal checklist, I fixated my eyes on the screen in front of me. *This time, I knew exactly what I was looking for.* Now, for the gently placed tube inside of me. There was light pressure, but I didn't focus on it much because I was going to see my baby girl! I listened intently to what my embryologist had to say.

"Okay, are we ready?"

And I was ready! I saw her! I spotted the tiny speck on the screen right away. I was so proud of myself!

I remained steady, not excited, not giddy, not anything. I could see the staff staring at me, waiting for the typical "Oh, I'm so excited" reaction. I was excited, so excited, but I was determined. As I lay there needing to pee, I just closed my eyes and listened to the humming in the dark room.

Later that evening, I sat on the patio watching the ocean waves, and tears just came down my face. I knew exactly what I just did, and as much as I wanted to suppress my emotions, I couldn't. I had locked them up for so long that there was clearly only one way out, and that's how they came out—in tears. Both Johnnie and I stood there staring over at the beautiful landscape of palm trees and blue ocean and held each other. We said nothing. I rested my head on his chest, listening to his heartbeat until I dozed off.

The following morning when we got to the airport, there was a mix-up with our tickets, so we were moved from sitting together. I was not happy at all about that. I demanded we sit together. Although the counter clerk seemed uninterested in helping, she finally caved and gave us the last two seats in the back of the plane by the restroom. All that mattered to me was we sat together.

Our flight to New York was five hours with no layovers, which was great compared to the last three flights. I put my headphones in and was hoping to just sleep and somehow drown out the consistent toilet flushing and unpleasant odor. We were enjoying a relatively smooth flight until things suddenly took a turn. It started with little turbulence, and feeling a few bumps, then a few body jerks from side to side. Before we knew it, we were being tossed around like socks in a dryer.

The pilot's voice crackled over the intercom, attempting to calm our nerves with the news that we were flying straight into a minor storm. "Minor storm?" I muttered, gripping the armrests with white knuckles. As if on cue, the turbulence intensified.

"Please stay seated with your seat belt on," the pilot urged, and in that moment, panic set in. Instinctively, I clutched my stomach, as if my grip could shield my unborn baby from the chaos unfolding around us.

Just when I thought things couldn't get any worse, the plane suddenly dropped from the sky. As I felt everything in my body come up toward my throat, I grabbed Johnnie's hand and instantly began to panic. The drop sent the overhead compartments flying open and passengers screaming in terror. I screamed so hard that I began to sob uncontrollably, all the while, holding my belly. All I could think was—*I don't want to lose this baby. I can't lose this baby!* I prayed as I was screaming, "Please God, I don't want to lose my baby again." The turbulence itself lasted about twenty minutes and my sobbing lasted the entire flight. My cries came with heavy panting, nausea, and a headache. The pain I felt rang in my stomach, and all I wanted to do was throw up.

I just knew I lost my baby girl.

All possibilities gone.

Once the flight had steadied everyone seemed comfortable going back to watching a movie, reading a book and drink service began. People began to get up to use the restroom, and as they did, they would pass my seat and see me crying. Some stopped and offered to hold my hand and say a prayer. One man walked by to remind me that we are safe now. Even the stewardess came by with a bottle of water and her personal cooling pad to help.

"It's ok now," others passed by and spoke. I even got a quick story of how "My wife and I have been on flights where it was much worse," told by an older gentleman.

It took roughly two hours from stepping off the plane to finally sinking into the comfort of our bed in our new Brooklyn apartment. The idea of having our own space offered a sense of solace, especially after the events of the day. As I lay there, tears streaming down my face, our new home enveloped us in the warmth and tranquility we desperately needed. That night, neither Johnnie nor I spoke a word. Instead, we lay side by side, lost in our own thoughts, grappling with the unimaginable.

Days turned into nights and so on. I found everything under the sun to keep my mind occupied. I remained in the loop regarding my retrieval progress with updates from the clinic. Out of the initial eight, only three successfully reached fertilization. The waiting game commenced, with approximately two weeks expected for the genetic testing results to arrive, coinciding with my own testing. We knew the drill.

Days dragged on, yet time was slipping away. On that 14th day, I woke up and thought—*Should I even take a test?* I lay there contemplating if it was even worth it. As I turned to throw the cover over my head, I locked eyes with Johnnie, "Well, we should try it. What will it do if it says what we already think we know?" he asked.

I got up a little reluctantly and prepared for my pregnancy test. My, how things had changed from last time. I looked at it and silently prayed, "God I don't know what you have in plan for me but please help me move forward after this. I can't do this anymore."

I took a seat and completed the routine task, leaving the pregnancy test stick on the bathroom counter as I exited the room, walked into the kitchen, made coffee, and mindlessly scrolled through Facebook. I then attempted to distract myself by organizing the clutter of pot spoons and spatulas in my drawers. I was trying to find anything to keep me busy and preoccupied and then my alarm chimed. It was time for the inevitable. I did the slow walk while peeling away the hang nail on my fingers. I tried to convince myself that if this is what I already know, it will be ok, and we can just get back to normal. Whatever normal is or will be. *It will be easier than before; this must be easier.*

I closed my eyes when I walked into the bathroom and a sudden jolt of pain shot through me as I clumsily bumped my funny bone. Was this a sign? Was I already feeling the sting of disappointment before it even happened? Rubbing the sore spot, I squinted with anticipation, bracing myself for the outcome. My Clearblue test read.

Pregnant!

"What the Fuck?" I yelled out.

"What, What, What?" Johnnie responded from the bedroom.

I walked out, staring at him, and said, "It says I'm pregnant! This can't be true!"

Johnnie jumped out of the bed to check the stick as well. "Go do another one. You have four boxes under the sink," he said.

I immediately gave him a dirty look, but then I thought it was a good idea. "But I can't pee right now. You think it would say something different after I drink water?"

"I don't know. Let's find out" he said.

I ran to the kitchen to chug a very large glass of water. I stared at that positive test while drinking. Thinking—*This can't be true!* But then my mind when to the dark side, *So, what happens when the next test is negative? What do I do then?* We were just so convinced it couldn't be right.

And here we go again! Timer on. Johnnie and I moved around like we were ants working on building our new home. We moved laundry, put dishes away, made the bed, cleaned our desk. Who knew you could accomplish all of this in a matter of minutes?

The alarm went off and we both paused. After what felt like an eternity, we fixed our clothing as if we needed to be presentable. And walked toward the bathroom. Johnnie stood by the door as I entered.

"Babe!" I walked out. "I have bad news."

"Really?" Johnnie asked with a disappointing face.

"It looks like you are going to have to be on diaper duty!"

I jumped on the bed, screaming and crying. We collapsed into each other's arms, hugging, and kissing.

We immediately called the clinic and told Dionne. She was just as excited as we were. I desperately needed to know our next steps. I was finally pregnant, and I needed to keep this baby.

Later that day, we received a follow-up email with which medications to continue and which to stop, what activities to avoid, and a little calendar, including my August 5th due date!

Wow!

Our next call was an 8:00 a.m. video chat with my mom.

"Mom, it worked! It worked!" Johnnie and I screamed, smiling on camera at her. She paused and immediately began to cry.

"I have been praying for this for a long time," she cried out.

We spent the day calling everyone who knew what we had been doing. I was clearly aware of the myth that it was bad luck to talk about a pregnancy before the first trimester was over, but this was just too exciting not to share. We had come so far, and everyone in our circle grieved with us before. They deserved to celebrate with us too.

We finally got some of that magical baby dust swirling all around us.

Chapter 31

Apple Blossom

That morning, after the crying-fest, Johnnie and I decided that our favorite breakfast spot—a cute little diner close to our home—would be the place for a celebratory meal. We stumbled in like party people, laughing and clinging to each other. We were giddy from our emotions and suddenly starving! The smell of sizzling bacon and freshly brewed coffee enveloped us as we entered.

I plopped down into a booth, rubbing my tired eyes. "I still can't believe it," I mumbled, my hands a little shaky, as I held the laminated menu in front of me.

Johnnie, wide-eyed and jittery, replied, "I know, right? Shitty diapers, late-night feedings, crying, and more crying, sleepless nights. It's going to be great! I'm just saying it's going to change our life... we're in for a wild ride, babe."

Afterward, he delved into the financial aspects of parenthood, listing the costs of essentials like food, diapers, and clothing. I was taken aback by his knowledge of these figures, acknowledging he has been on this path too, but I shot him a warning glance, urging him not to ruin the moment. Meeting my gaze, he responded with a reassuring smile.

Our waitress, a cheerful woman with a perpetual smile, approached us. "Good morning! Ready to order?"

And we were. While I rattled off my favorite breakfast choices, Johnnie began with a series of jokes at the table, making the waitress chuckle as she scribbled down our order. When she walked away, Johnnie turned to me with a mischievous glint in his eye. "I guess we're officially entering the realm of dad jokes. I am so excited!"

I realized that Johnnie's excitement for this baby really matched mine. Between pancake bites and coffee sips, we started discussing what would happen next. So many questions—*Does my diet change again?*

"Babe, wait, I heard you can't have sushi or deli meant, soft cheeses, or wine when you're pregnant. Is that true?"

As the waitress returned, she overheard us bickering about sushi, and deli meat and asked, "Is this your first?"

I looked up at her and said, "YES!"

I heard how loud and excited my voice was but didn't care. She smiled, topped off our waters, and said it would be magical. I thought about that for a while. *Magical—will it be magical? What's magic about it? When does the magic begin? Does the magic start now? Is the magic in the baby dust?*

With full stomachs and our hearts still fluttering, Johnnie grabbed the check, but looked up in surprise.

"On the house," he declared, showing me the handwritten note on the check.

The waitress came by and chuckled, "Congratulations! You will be great parents!"

Over the next several weeks, Johnnie and I found ourselves facing the impending reality of parenthood like two deer caught in the headlights. First-time parents! Panic mode initiated. *What do I do? Where do I start? Is there a manual for this? Is there a class for sleeping with your eyes open? Do I practice swaddling now? Can Johnnie be my practice model?*

And breastfeeding! How do I go about that without feeling like a human vending machine? Is there a lactation consultant out there who can teach me how to breastfeed discreetly in public, or do I need to start practicing with a blanket draped over my head like a magician?

Oh, and what about the legendary "sleep when the baby sleeps" advice? Does that include napping in the middle of the grocery store? Is that what moms do? Holy shit!

Days following, I was armed with my little arsenal of pregnancy essentials. I diligently popped my vitamins, and meds that were still required for me to use up to my 2nd trimester. I created a regimen and followed it to the T all while embracing the chaos of New York, winter storms, traffic, and encounters with moody transit employees. I made it a habit to turn everything negative around me into something positive. I made myself this promise.

Swollen feet? A sign of a baby brewing.

Moody transit employees? Practice patience for gentle parenting.

And yes, the inability to enjoy coffee, wine, cheese, and sushi meant my baby was destined to be worldly.

The most heartwarming and euphoric feeling washed over me this time-the magic of Christmas this year for me. It's a holiday deeply ingrained in my heart and filled with cherished memories from childhood. In recent years, the enchantment seemed to have faded, but this year was different.

In early childhood, I had this weird aversion to anything apple related. Was it some unresolved childhood trauma or a psychological quirk? Who knows! But pregnancy had other plans for me. Suddenly, apples were all I craved. I needed apples for breakfast, lunch, and dinner. I dreamt about apples. I even needed apples in the middle of a New York (the big apple, pun intended) blizzard.

In early 2018, New York City experienced a significant winter storm that brought heavy snowfall, strong winds, and frigid temperatures to the region. They called it the "bomb cyclone." So, like the pregnant apple lunatic I was, I politely, yet aggressively, told Johnnie he had to brave the storm to get them for me. I laid under a warm blanket, TV lights flickering, as I watched him gear up like he was about to conquer Mount Everest, snowboarding jacket on, boots, gloves, hat, scarf, and goggles and into the cold he went.

About an hour later, I watched him as he huffed and puffed shaking off the cold. "The man at the market asked if I was crazy," he said, shivering and slightly annoyed. "He had to go in the back of the store where there is no heat to see if he had any apples, and he told me winter isn't apple season and this blizzard he hasn't gotten any produce delivery. I didn't have the energy to tell him my wife is pregnant, crazy, and testing my patience."

I snatched the tiniest apples he could get out of his hands, disregarding the frosty adventure he had, and devoured them like I'd never seen food before. After a while, our local grocer knew to have at least three apples on deck for Johnnie to pick up.

As my belly gradually grew, excitement surged through me. The New York winter disguised my burgeoning bump with coats and sweaters, but the big reveal would be coming in the spring.

Amidst the excitement of pregnancy, my mind was filled with dreams— dreams of a blissful family, echoing laughter, and the joy of future grandchildren. Yet, alongside these hopeful visions, there lingered a shadow of fear.

Terrifying nightmares of losing my baby girl before even holding her. A simple walk down the street became fraught with imagined dangers, as I instinctively cradled my growing belly, bracing for the worst. Every unexpected movement or encounter triggered a surge of panic, turning everyday moments into harrowing nightmares.

Once, on a crowded train, a sudden jolt sent my heart racing as visions of falling on my belly flooded my mind. My exaggerated flinch caught the attention of a kind elderly woman who offered me her seat.

I was determined to have a positive mindset, nothing else, but that sometimes was hard. As my body underwent physical changes, my appetite grew, and my mental fatigue all kicked in at the same time. Johnnie's work demanded more of his time and attention, and I required more of him as well.

We understood the importance of his business trips, even though it meant he would be away often. I was scared that I couldn't handle this pregnancy on my own, but our family and friends reassured me they would be there the whole time.

One morning, while Johnnie was on a business trip to Los Angeles, the day started off like any other, until a routine trip to the bathroom took a turn. As I sat there, I could feel three large blood clots coming out of me. My heart raced. *What was happening?* In complete distress, I called Johnnie, waking him up at 5:00 a.m. PST, and my voice fluttering in sheer panic in a plea for answers.

"What does this mean?" I cried out. "Why? No! Why?"

"Babe don't panic. We need to get you to a doctor," he reassured me.

"How? Who will see me on a Sunday?" I shot back.

At this point, I hadn't even picked a gynecologist yet.

We both frantically searched our good friend Google for a doctor available on a Sunday. Johnnie, relentless in his determination, called numerous places, encountering only voicemails and unanswered calls. My hands trembled, my heart pounded, and my gaze remained fixated on those distressing clots in the toilet. I couldn't bring myself to flush them away, unsure of the gravity of the situation.

At around noon, as I lay on my bed looking over at the bathroom toilet sipping a cup of tea and panicking, relief came in the form of a call from Johnnie. "Babe, I found you a doctor. They're expecting you now. Get dressed and go; I have an Uber on the way." Tear-streaked and shaken, I dressed hastily, and as promised, an Uber waiting for me outside. Through the streets of Park Slope, Brooklyn, my mind raced with self-blame. *What had I done wrong? Did that accidental sip of Johnnie's wine trigger this? Did I eat something or miss my vitamins? I was tormenting myself with 'what ifs' and blaming myself for this situation, as I had done before.*

The doctor Johnnie found turned out to be at an urgent care facility. Check-in was swift, and they had all my information ready, a testament to Johnnie's efficient coordination. The doctor was a seemingly kind middle-aged man, and I was soon to learn also a father of five. While lying on the examination table he asked.

"How far along are you?"

"I'm eight weeks," I replied.

"Let's check for a heartbeat before we proceed" he said.

Thump. Thump. *Ahh*. There it was—the sound of a healthy heartbeat. "You're pregnant, my nurse told me hubby was nervous because of a blood clot? Everything seems good here, but you need to see your OB immediately," he stated.

Relief washed over me, and I quickly called Johnnie to share the news. Silence enveloped our conversation, punctuated only by his audible sniffles. I didn't want to talk about it further that night as I just laid in bed, slowly rubbing my bell.

Monday morning found me at a new doctor's office, undergoing ultrasounds, heartbeat checks, and bloodwork. All results came back normal, so the true nature of the blood clots remained elusive. Explanations mattered less than the reassurance that my baby was safe and still with me.

After that, I did everything with patience and self-awareness. I walked slowly; I paid attention to what foods I ate. I was a complete nervous wreck, I trained myself in meditation. I had to quiet my thoughts and mind. On an elevator ride up to my apartment, my neighbor, who had a toddler at home whom I could hear every day when I walked out of the elevator, made small talk with me for the first time.

"How many weeks are you? Do you hate your life yet?" She asked.

I looked over at her smiled and nodded while rubbing my belly. "I have no reason to hate my life."

I could see by her look she was not fond of my answer, but it wasn't for her to judge my life and my feelings, and I didn't really care what she had to say. No judgment from my end, but you could say we never became those friendly New York neighbors. It was unfortunate, as we were just a door away, but it seemed like motherhood meant something totally different for her than it did for me.

As I navigated the unfamiliar pregnancy territory, adjusting to my changing body, and delving into the pages of the gift given to me by Melissa, another of my sisters-in-law, "What to Expect When You're Expecting," I found myself immersed in the daunting task of choosing the right obstetrician. I liked the one I had seen after the blood clots but wanted to keep looking.

Despite meticulously combing through numerous reviews of doctors, the perfect fit remained intangible. It felt like I'd been on a blind date with the entire medical profession, and none of them had sparked that magical something. After investing so much time in the quest for the ideal fertility specialist, I knew I couldn't give up. This precious baby deserved nothing but the best, and the search continued.

Not long after three medical breakups, I met Dr. Savoy. She was tall and commanding in her three-inch heels; her hair and makeup would impress any runway model, and her perfectly pressed pants and tailored doctor's coat practically screamed, "I am the woman on your stock photos website." Initially, she struck me as a bit of a brick wall—stoic, bordering on off-putting. She spoke to me very directly and to the point. When she did smile, it seemed like she was doing me a favor. *Where were the warm fuzzy feelings I desperately craved?*

I complained about her to Johnnie for weeks, trying to find flaws, but I was mostly criticizing her direct personality. Funny, Johnnie saw something I didn't, even when he let out some inappropriate joke, and she didn't respond like most. He still felt she was just the right fit for us.

"Why do you like her? She doesn't laugh at your jokes like everyone else does!"

"She does!"

"Ah, no, she doesn't!"

"I see it. You are just a little sensitive and a bit hormonal," he'd say, his voice laced with gentle amusement. "You're missing the point. She's a straight shooter and providing you with all the information you need. Isn't that what you wanted?"

His words resonated with me. Maybe my hormonal haze had clouded my judgment. Maybe Dr. Savoy, for all her apparent coldness, was exactly the no-nonsense doctor I needed to navigate this complex journey. So, I took a leap of faith and kept her as my doctor. And Johnnie was 100% right. She may not have been all warm smiles and fuzzy hugs, but her competence and expertise proved invaluable. And as the weeks turned into months, I even started to appreciate her dry wit and quiet confidence.

Things were looking good. Spring was in the air, and I was growing, and glowing and my baby girl was thriving. We picked out names, put our registry together, visited multiple baby stores, checked out strollers, cribs, swaddles, car seats. I was feeling good and felt we had everything under control for an August baby.

Now, at 25 weeks, I was preparing to celebrate my birthday. I was turning 42 years old in July. My love for Christmas comes second only to my love for my birthday, and this year was a big one for so many obvious reasons. Johnnie was away for work again and according to him it was a good idea to be around family to keep an eye on me. I was feeling fine to be on my own, but it was nice to spend time with my mom—those moments were exactly what I needed. As my family and I gathered around the dining table, we discussed my birthday plans and the level of celebration I felt up to. Would it be a lively "whoo girl" party, or a more subdued sit-down dinner? My mom suggested a sit-down affair around 6 p.m. As laughter filled the room at my expense, with old people jokes, and being an older mom. As one of those jokes made me laugh so hard I suddenly had the urge to use the bathroom, again.

At this stage, I saw the toilet about 20 times daily, but this time, I felt a little weird. As I sat there holding onto the bathroom sink to ease myself down, I felt a pain in my stomach and could feel large clots coming out of me. I became frantic and screamed for my mom.

She came rushing in and became frantic as well. She then immediately ran out and called my brother Kris and his wife. All I could think was, please, please don't let this be a miscarriage. While I overheard everyone outside of the bathroom door talking about the situation, I just needed to talk to Johnnie. My rock, my stead place. I needed him. I yelled out to my brother to call him, while I slowly pushed my body up from the toilet, I kept asking, "Why was this happening again?"

Whatever was discussed between both Johnnie and Kris, in a matter of minutes there was a game plan for me. My brother and mom walked me three blocks to a women's health clinic. Apparently, my brother's good friend had worked at the front counter, and he had a plan to just walk in and convince them to get me in without an appointment.

My mom sat beside me in the waiting room. It wasn't just any medical facility; it was a family planning clinic a place where women could seek various forms of reproductive healthcare, including abortions. As I looked around, I couldn't help but notice the diversity of women present, vibrant mix of Dominican, Puerto Rican, Cuban, and Caribbean- all coming together for their health needs. This clinic isn't just a building; it's a vital part of our community. Today, it remains crucial for women seeking specialized medical attention related to female reproductive health. Its existence speaks volumes about the ongoing need for inclusive and accessible healthcare options.

As I had completed my surveying of the room, I was back looking at my brother, to see him give me the head nod that I was in. My mom and I sat there and waited and waited and waited some more. For three hours we waited. My brother left and periodically came back with snacks and water for us. There was an undiscussed understanding that this space was for women who needed help and with that help meant patience. Finally, my name was called, and my mom and I hurried in. The nurses did the regular routine by checking my weight, temperature, blood pressure, and oxygen levels. Then, it was off to a hard plastic seat to ask me questions.

"What are you in for?" the not-so-pleasant nurse asked with a Caribbean accent.

"I am 25 weeks pregnant, and today I dropped two blood clots. This has happened before. I need to see if there is a heartbeat, please," I pleaded.

"Well, before we get to that, are you on any medication?" she asked.

"Yes. I am. I am on vitamins and soon to be my last round of meds for my fertility treatment."

While I rattled off all the medications and my routine, the nurse paused and asked to be excused. I looked over at my mom with a face of curiosity. About two minutes later she hurried back to the little desk and then asked us to follow her to the doctor's office. When she ushered us in to a small room, we were met withs two women standing near a counter filled with plastic gloves, syringes, and medical tools. The first doctor seemed to look like she was in her early 30's, slim, with long blonde hair. The other was an older woman with curly brown hair. Her mannerism and tone came off as if she was the expert or veteran of the clinic. They asked us both my mom and I to have a seat. I then immediately called Johnnie and put him on the speakerphone to hear what they wanted to talk about so urgently.

I gazed up at them, desperation etched across my face, and I whispered, "I just need to see if there is a heartbeat right now. That is all I am here for."

With a stern demeanor, the older woman replied, "I understand you want to hear the heartbeat, and we will get to that, but first, we want to talk to you about the medication you are taking. I think you need to stop those immediately."

Turning to my mother for support, I then locked my eyes with the doctor. "I am sorry. Are you a fertility specialist?" I asked.

"No, but I see pregnant women here all day long and from my experience this list of medicine is not good."

At that moment, I was acutely aware of my surroundings—and of their roles. Frustration bubbling within, I asserted, "All I need is to see if there is a heartbeat."

"Well, Mandy, as your doctor, I have to recommend you stop taking those medications immediately," she insisted.

"You are not my doctor, and if you were, you would know my husband and I have been trying to have a baby for almost ten years. I am finally pregnant, and I need to stay pregnant. Unless you are a fertility specialist or my doctor, I will not be stopping these meds until my doctors say so. If they told me I had to do a fuckin' rain dance to have this baby, I would do it. So, all I need you to do is check for a fucking heartbeat. Can you do that?"

Pure shock was written all over their faces. The older woman turned to the nurse and uttered, "Okay, let's listen to the baby's heartbeat."

Finally, the heartbeat was checked. And there was again a heartbeat! I sighed a deep breath of relief. *But why was this happening again?* Overwhelmed by the interminable wait and the relentless back-and-forth, I found that six hours had stealthily slipped away. When we walked out of the clinic, shops had closed, and it was nighttime. I couldn't shake off the worry about the prolonged wait for the baby's heartbeat. Had it altered anything in my pregnancy?

My mom and I strolled home, holding hands. "There is still a heartbeat, Mandy," she whispered, a refrain of solace as if weaving a mantra to ward off the shadows. "I need you to find a way to reduce your stress levels. You looked like you were about to explode. I understand that you are scared, and I am, too, but stress can cause more issues. Please, I am begging you to relax."

Silent echoes reverberated between us. An agreement eluded my trembling lips. She sensed my silence. It's incredibly difficult to find peace and be stress-free when the possibility of losing your baby is always in the back of your mind, especially after all that we have already been through.

I gave my mom a hug and hopped into an Uber for a long, traffic-ridden ride to Brooklyn, which I was okay with. I needed some time to myself, and I needed to fill Johnnie in. My frustration with the doctor led me to hang up on Johnnie abruptly earlier and I didn't answer his multiple calls afterward, as I was too busy with my irate request for heartbeat check. Fortunately, he spoke with my mom while I was in the restroom and had some updates. He was not mad at me, just concerned. It became clear that for that short period my mom was on the phone with him she shared how concerned she was about my stress levels, and he also reiterated her sentiments.

Before this, I felt very proud of myself for practicing the little tips my therapist shared, my quick online meditation teaching, my yoga in the morning, and my positive repetitive mantras. I was eating right, staying hydrated, and taking vitamins. *What more could I do?* I knew in my heart I was doing everything I could.

Still, time went by, and that was the last of the clots thankfully. As the temperature warmed up, I spent more days in the sun, doing lots of walking with Johnnie in the parks, in the neighborhood—anywhere I could walk I did—all while staring at the multiple ultrasound pictures of our baby and her growth.

And time finally seemed to be on my side.

Chapter 32

Beautiful Vision

As I entered my 30th week of pregnancy, the routine "non-stress tests" (NST) at my birthing hospital Brooklyn Methodist became a regular part of my routine. Initially, they were just appointments I had to check off my list, but over time, they transformed into something more meaningful.

Some days, the walk to the hospital felt like a pilgrimage, but I pushed through with my baby playlist that I listened to repeatedly. My song choices went from Creed's "Arms Wide Open" to Lauryn Hill's "To Zion" to U2's "Beautiful Day"—and my favorite of them all—Beyonce's "Love on Top." These songs helped me in different ways—some days I cried while I listened and other days, I was incredibly energized.

The first two weeks of these appointments were a bit tedious. Sitting there for twenty minutes, hooked up to machines, felt like nothing but a mundane task. But then something changed. I started noticing the familiar faces of the nurses, and they began recognizing me too. Soon, our interactions evolved from clinical to personal. We swapped stories about life, shared a few laughs, and even bonded over our love for sweet treats. At every appointment, they were there, not just as medical professionals but as cheerleaders for us. Their smiles, laughter, and encouraging words became pillars of strength for me to lean on whenever I needed.

These visits eventually turned into mini celebrations, as I would bring in boxes of cupcakes and donuts. They deserved that and so much more. They were on the front lines of helping ease soon-to-be moms' pain and suffering—and there was a lot of it. I would bring them the whole damn bakery if I could!

However, everything changed during my 34th week appointment—ironically, the day before my birthday. What was supposed to be a routine morning test, followed by an appointment to get my hair blown out and a nice relaxing pedicure for a pre-birthday dinner, turned into something unexpected and worrisome. My nerves and sense of excitement turned quickly into intense fear. I had no idea what would happen next.

As I scanned the room, I immediately noticed the familiar faces missing that day. But more than that, the atmosphere just felt different. The nurses were moving about silently, with minimal chit-chat, a departure from the usual lively exchanges I had grown accustomed to. I introduced myself to the intake nurse, my voice filled with excitement, but her response was more subdued.

The absence of the usual energy was palpable, leaving me slightly disheartened. I turned my attention to my phone, texting friends and scrolling through random Facebook posts, while talking to Johnnie about our evening plans. A few minutes later a nurse walked in with concern written all over her face. She began to reset my test multiple times without any explanation whatsoever.

I watched closely as she meticulously adjusted the equipment, her eyes rapidly reviewing the ripped paper coming out of the meter, and again readjusting cords. At first, I thought maybe I was just sitting the wrong way preventing her from getting a good reading. So, I adjusted myself, all while trying to look over her shoulder to read the random dots on the graph. I couldn't shake the uneasy feeling building inside me. I finally gathered the courage to ask what was happening. Her response sent a chill down my spine. "I will have to have your doctor speak with you," she said quietly, her eyes filled with concern.

Johnnie and I looked over at each other. He immediately stood up and walked over to the nurses' station to ask what was happening.

"Sir, we have a wheelchair coming for your wife, and we will escort her to labor and delivery," I overheard her saying. I immediately jumped off my bed still connected to my monitoring cables, butterflies fluttering in my stomach.

"It's not time! She is due in August. What is happening?" I called out.

Suddenly, a soft-spoken nurse came around the corner, held my hand, and said in a soft voice, "There were some irregularities with your tests, and we have contacted your doctor, who is waiting for you in labor and delivery. It will be a few minutes before the wheelchair is up so you could walk if you are up to it or wait."

"I can walk." I responded back quickly.

I stood there impatiently waiting for the nurse to detach the monitor hooked on to me and then immediately grabbed my bag hastily gripped Johnnie's hand. Sitting there any longer made no sense seeing that they provided me with limited to no information. I needed to know exactly what these irregularities were.

"Which way do we go?" I abruptly asked.

My heart was pounding with uncertainty. I felt a wave of unease wash over me. Each step felt heavy. We walked down a long dimly lit corridor with no signs or postings, it felt like we were just walking into a void. I took deep breaths and small steps. As we rounded a corner, a counter materialized before us. A stern-faced woman, her eyes sharp behind thick glasses, asked for my band on my wrist, scrutinizing it like a secret decoder ring.

"Good, we have been preparing for you."

My heart lurched. Preparing for what? Panic welled up inside me, as I white knuckled Johnnie's hand, and then began to breathe heavily. She ushered us into a sterile room where a cold metal bed awaited. The nurse, whom I dubbed Nurse Iceberg in my head, instructed me to change into a gown.

"Put your belongings in here, you may be here for a while," she commanded, her voice clipped, all while handing me a plastic bag.

I did as I was told, then sat on the edge of the bed, feeling increasingly like a helpless bird, blinking unconsciously. I watched her move around my body, attaching cords and tape all over. Wires snaked around my belly like a miniature jungle gym while a tiny monitor beeped and blooped like a chorus of anxious frogs.

Just then, Dr. Savoy entered, her brow furrowed in concern. "What's going on here?" she asked, staring directly at me.

I stared back confused. Just then, Nurse Iceberg handed her an iPad and said, "We paged you after the first EFM. There's a troubling correlation between her contractions and the baby's heartbeat."

"What is she talking about? I don't feel any contractions!" I exclaimed, my voice rising in a mixture of fear and confusion. "How do we stop them and what about the baby's heartbeat?"

Dr. Savoy's gaze met mine, a serious expression settling on her face. "Your results show we probably need to deliver the baby today," she said calmly.

"But it's too early!" I protested. "And we've been planning for a natural birth!"

Johnnie rose to his feet, his demeanor assertive yet respectful. "Doctor," he began, "is there still a possibility for a natural birth at this stage? We're so close to the due date. What are the advantages and disadvantages of an immediate delivery?"

Dr. Savoy's expression softened as she considered his question. "We can continue monitoring for a while," she conceded, "but if the contractions escalate, we may have to reassess.

Mandy's contractions are occurring, even though she may not feel them, as they momentarily affect the baby's heart rate. The advantage of immediate delivery would ensure the baby's safety, but it deviates from your birth plan and may pose challenges with breastfeeding. Like any surgery, there are inherent risks. Why don't we keep our eyes on the contractions..."

I nodded, my heart pounding against my ribs. The doctor's words echoed in my ears. As she prepared to leave, I blurted out, "tomorrow's my birthday!"

She paused, and a smile finally broke through her stoic façade, "Well then," she said, her voice softening, "this will be the best birthday gift ever."

Tears welled up in my eyes as I looked at Johnnie. He pulled me close and said, "We needed to let our families know what is happening."

He immediately began texting, as I lay on the bed, staring at the ceiling, searching for an inner calm that seemed miles away. Each beep and bloop of the monitor felt like a hammer blow to my nerves. All I could try to do was focus on controlling my breathing, willing my body to relax and cooperate. I kept wondering was this all my fault. *Were the blood clots a sign? Was it my age? Did I do this to our little girl?* I could not stop thinking this was all my fault.

As we sat in a daze of the monotonous hum of machines and occasional rustle of paperwork, a nurse would materialize like a phantom, flitting in to scrutinize my scans, take my vitals, and then vanish without a word.

After what felt like an eternity, a burly male nurse with a booming voice and a smile that could melt glaciers announced, "Alright, folks! Time for our star of the show to take the stage!" He clapped his hands once, the sound echoing in the sterile silence. "We're moving you up to your pre-labor room, where they'll be prepping you for the big event! Hmm another geriatric pregnancy, seems like I have a few of these today?"

My jaw dropped. "Surgery? What? Geriatric, what the fuck are you talking about?" I sputtered, indignation rising like bile in my throat. My nerves were so wrecked I couldn't ask questions patiently or politely.

The orderly chuckled, "Don't worry, we got you. You can talk to your doctor when we get to your room."

Then he tried his best to make the walk and the elevator ride entertaining, and as much as I appreciated what he was saying, I just could not join in on his positivity. I remained quiet the entire time, finally the elevator doors whooshed open, revealing a brightly lit hallway that led to a room bathed in sunlight. It looked more like a luxury hotel suite than a hospital room, complete with a plush-sized bed, a flat-screen TV tuned to ESPN, and a cozy couch where Johnnie plopped himself on, testing its comfort.

Not soon after, I was making myself comfortable in the room when Dr. Savoy entered, her face a mask of professional calm. "So," she began, her voice a low hum, "we've decided to expedite your delivery. You'll be receiving an epidural shortly, and we aim to have this little one in your arms within the next few hours."

Tears welled up in my eyes, blurring my vision. "What's happening?" I croaked, my voice thick with emotion. Johnnie stood up to stand by my side as the doctor walked closer.

She placed a gentle hand on mine. "Your contractions are getting closer together. As that happens, oxygen is deprived for the baby, and the longer we wait, the greater the risk." She pointed to a monitor displaying a series of jagged lines. "See these spikes? They coincide with your contractions, and your baby's heartbeat drops momentarily when they occur. It's only a few seconds, but it's a risk we can't afford to take."

Her stoic facade momentarily crumbled, revealing a flicker of sympathy in her eyes. "I understand this is scary," she admitted, her voice softening, "I know you're scared.

This is a scary process. I have three children of my own, and I know as a mom, we have set views and ideas of what we want, and you want this baby. You told me so. You told me how long you have tried for this baby. She is ready to come out into the world. I promise I will do everything I can to make this smooth and safe, and you will have a healthy baby girl for your birthday."

She squeezed my hand; a gesture of unexpected warmth this was the first time I saw beyond her professional façade. As she was making her way out, she asked if I was okay and if I needed anything. I told her we had come in at 8:00 am for the stress test and now it was 5:00 p.m. and I was starving. She looked at Johnnie and turned her stoic voice back on,

"You better get your butt across the street and get her food asap. She cannot have food two hours before the epidural."

Johnnie bounced up and down, grabbed his phone, kissed me, and ran out. I could see a small tear from his eye fall. He was feeling just as stressed and emotional as I was, but he kept it together. Now, his job was to get me food.

After a few minutes the doctor came back in with a nurse, her eyes scanning the monitors like a hawk.

"Where's Johnnie?" she demanded; her voice clipped.

My stomach rumbled, a hollow echo in the silence. "He's not back yet," I managed to say, feeling a wave of helplessness wash over me.

The doctor's lips pursed into a thin line. "Well, he better hurry."

I immediately grabbed my phone to call him, "Babe, the doctor said to hurry your ass back here." I laughed out loud, hearing him panting.

"I'm trying to hurry, but these assholes are taking forever! Hey dude, can you hurry up with that burger and fries? My wife is about to give birth, and she needs this immediately."

While I waited for some sustenance to fill my emptiness. I also craved comforting words to help me process this uncertainty. The first person I thought of was my mother.

I had to hear her voice, I had to hear her say it would be ok.

"Hi," I said very low and slowly.

"I am on my way, Mandy. Your brother Robin and I will be there soon," she responded in a rushed tone. It sounded like she was gathering herself to leave the house in a panic and didn't have the time to hear what I was searching for. So as much as I wanted to hear something, I wanted her here more. I hung up and scrolled for another familiar voice that could give me what I so needed.

I then called my dad, seeking refuge in his wisdom and strength, hoping his words would offer the reassurance I desperately needed. He spoke of pride and resilience, and assured me that everything would be alright, it didn't help me feel any better. I wasn't sure what words I was searching for. There probably were not any consoling words for me at that point. What I truly longed for was to transcend this moment of fear and uncertainty and to hold my precious baby girl in my arms.

About twenty minutes later, Johnnie rushed in panting and sweating profusely, with a greasy bag. It had to be the best cold food I have had.

As we sat there waiting for the epidural, my mind began to race. I grabbed the remote and turned the TV off. There was something burning inside of me that needed to be said and it had to be now.

"Babe, we need to talk," I said, quivering in my voice.

He stood up and walked over to the window and looked over as the sun began to set.

"What's up, babe?" he asked.

"When we go into delivery, and our baby girl enters this world, I need you to be everywhere she is—anywhere the nurses and doctors take her, you go with her. You make sure she is safe. I will be ok. I need you to promise me this. You will make sure they take care of her, do all the necessary testing, and they need to tell you everything they are doing for her. You are her advocate. Tell me you will do that."

My voice resonated with both urgency and fear as I looked at him, pleading for his commitment. "Johnnie," I called out, waiting anxiously for his response. He sat in silence for a moment, his thoughts visibly swirling in his mind, as the weight of my words settled between us.

He looked up at me, hands pressed together. "Everything will be ok," he said quietly.

It wasn't the response I wanted, but I knew he heard me, and he would do everything he had to make sure our family was safe.

Just then, a slender figure materialized in the doorway, casting a shadow engulfing the room in an even deeper gloom. "Mrs. Refvik," he announced, his voice carrying of a seasoned professional. "May I see your wrist, please?"

I rattled off my name and date of birth, the words tumbling out of my mouth with an uncharacteristic lack of grace. Each time I had to repeat them, the fear tightened its grip on me, turning my voice into a nervous tremor.

"I'll be administering your epidural," he continued, his tone devoid of warmth. "Please relax, take deep breaths, and try to stay as still as possible. Mr. Refvik, you may stand here and hold her hand for support."

The room fell silent. Every muscle in my body was taut with anticipation, the fear paralyzing me. I desperately wanted to laugh, cough, and break the oppressive silence, but a primal instinct kept me rooted in place.

"I'll be working near your spine," he said, his voice a low murmur, "Please take small, shallow breaths and avoid any movement."

As the procedure began, each prick of the needle felt like a betrayal, a violation of my fragile sense of control. I focused on stillness, my entire being concentrated on remaining perfectly immobile.

Only my eyes dared to move, darting around the room in a desperate search for anything to distract me. I just wanted to crumble into Johnnie's arms whenever I looked at him. I clung to his hand—his warmth. His presence was my lifeline.

I tried to close my eyes, to conjure an image of my daughter, the precious life growing within me. But the picture remained stubbornly blank, replaced by an emptiness.

Finally! We were done with that! He taped my back, checked all my monitors, and said "Your doctor would be in with you shortly."

It seemed like my doctor was eavesdropping because she immediately walked in. "We are going to begin prepping you for the C-section," she said, adding that another doctor, nurses, and an anesthesiologist would be with me.

"You're in excellent hands," she continued.

Not long after, I was in a surgical room. Johnnie was told to put scrubs on from head to toe. (He has gotten comfortable in scrubs in the past few years.) We smiled at each other, nervous and excited. They asked me to lie down for the anesthesiologist to prepare me. I looked over at Johnnie and he leaned down for a kiss. I whispered to him, "Babe, whatever happens, you follow our baby girl."

He looked at me, kissed me, and said, "Yes, babe, but nothing is going to happen. We are all good. I know we are."

We held each other's hands as we watched the doctors prep a curtain on my waist. All I could see were their heads moving around me. I could hear medical instruments clanging, and although I had some pain meds, I could smell burning. It became stronger and stronger like metal. Then, I could hear the doctor's voice. Nurses stood at the side of me, next to a small incubator. All of them wore masks and gloves. My eyes darted around, but I stayed focused on Johnnie's face. Every so often, the anesthesiologists confirmed I was ok. Not too long after, I heard Dr. Savoy ask, "Are you ready to meet your baby girl? Did you pick a name yet?"

"Yes, we did! Her name is Riley!" I blurted out through tears.

I looked over at Johnnie and smiled. For days, we went back and forth with names. He wanted something that symbolized his Irish heritage since his mom had passed, and her heritage meant a lot to her. This name represented "valiant," which means boldly courageous, brave, or determined, especially in the face of difficulty or danger.

Riley was perfect. She was considered last on the list of possibilities to get us pregnant. She made it through that horrible plane drop. She remained strong and stayed with me through the multiple scares. She had been showing herself to me for years.

Both Johnnie and I were elated. Tears streamed down both our faces when Riley was put into our hands.

Moments later, the nurses, along with Johnnie took her over to the little incubator and began to clean her up, checking her vitals and size.

I could hear light cries and my heart melted. A nurse hurriedly wrapped up Riley and brought over to me to get a kiss and a quick picture. I was instantly in love. And then it was time to close the incision and go under anesthesia. I held Johnnie's hand, told him I loved him, and told him to give Riley another kiss for me. I closed my eyes and said a prayer, asking that I would wake up after this to hold my little girl.

Later I woke up in the recovery room and as I slowly gained focus, I could see Johnnie in the distance, but I didn't see Riley. He started to slowly walk over to me. I tried to look around him for her and immediately began to panic. "Johnnie where is she?" I asked with a quiver in my voice.

"She is perfect and perfectly alright; I came over to see how you were doing. Calm down babe, she is healthy and so amazing. She is the most beautiful person I have ever seen." He said with so much happiness in his voice.

Moments later a nurse walked over and said, "Hi mom, are you ready to hold this most precious beautiful baby girl?" With a nod, I masked the sheer elation that threatened to burst forth, keeping my overwhelming joy a secret for just a moment longer. Tears of joy welled up in my eyes as my lips quivered with overwhelming happiness, and my hands trembled with anticipation. I fought to contain the powerful emotions surging through me, desperate to hold my precious baby in my arms. But it couldn't be contained any longer. I stood there crying while holding my baby girl.

"Happy Birthday to you Riley it's your birthday, and guess what? Tomorrow is mommies." It was the greatest and most precious gift I ever got!

I recalled gazing down at her face, enveloped in a sense of déjà vu that echoed through each vision I held of her. Her soft brown hair and the depth of her big brown eyes felt achingly familiar. The way she looked at me, a gaze that connected us a bond so real.

"My guardian angel, you have been watching over me for a long time."

I whispered, as I kissed her forehead.

Epilogue

As I reflect on our journey, I can't help but feel a sense of awe at the experiences that morphed together to shape our lives. Our daughter, our little shining star, continues to light up our world with her boundless energy and voracious curiosity.

Her name, meaning valiant and strong, couldn't be more fitting. She embraces each day with a zest for life that inspires us all. She often asks about the story of her birth, and we excitedly share about the journey full of obstacles at every turn, our passion and determination that never wavered. We were brave adventurers, driven by a love already forming in our hearts … and a vision of a beautiful little girl with brown eyes and brown hair in my spirit.

There is an interesting saying that a child born to a parent over the age of 40 is considered your guardian angel. Whether it's wisdom beyond her years or a strong sense of purpose, our daughter embodies these traits and more, reminding us daily of life's precious gifts.

When she turned one, we embarked on another new chapter, hoping to expand our family. Unfortunately, that chapter ended with the loss of a potential sibling, bringing heartache once again upon us. I was confronted with pain and grief during secondary infertility. It took time to heal but the one glimmer of hope was the little one I held in my arms. She gave me strength, which allowed me to become an advocate and support others, and in turn, this helped me.

In continuing with and moving forward, Johnnie and I decided that our path to honoring our losses (embryos) would be to name them. One ritual we did for years, was at the dinner table where we would call out their names and say how proud we were of them. Brooklyn (she), our oldest, would be the writer, and Crow (he) would see the world for all its wonder and share it with others. And our youngest, Laken (she), would turn everything upside down to make sure it was right. What we loved the most about these names were that they shared a common thread; they are all derived from natural elements of the Earth. On Diwali, known as the Festival of Lights, a significant Hindu celebration symbolizing the victory of light over darkness the three of us light candles and say a special prayer to each of them.

We channel our love and energy toward our family, our community and causes close to our hearts. United in purpose, Johnnie and I embarked on a mission to empower young people battling diabetes, culminating in the creation of "The SugarCube" app—an innovative tool to ease the management of this condition.

Through it all, our belief in the transformative power of science, technology and prayer has not only enriched our lives but also allowed us to make a meaningful impact on the world around us. As we continue this journey, we embrace each day with gratitude, humor, and a deep-seated conviction that every challenge is an opportunity for growth and every setback a chance to rise stronger than before.

A Note from the Author

I want to extend a heartfelt thank you to you, the reader, for joining me on this part of my journey. I also want to acknowledge that while I share my own experiences and insights on these pages, it's important to note that I am not a doctor or specialist. Rather, my perspectives are shaped by my personal journey and the lessons I learned along the way.

In this book, I invite you to step into my world and understand the motivations behind this narrative, as I believe deeply in the power of storytelling to foster understanding and empathy.

I would be remiss not to acknowledge that I decided to document my experiences years after concluding fertility treatments, fully aware of the advancements in technology and medical practices since then. My experiences were at a certain time and in a certain place. Still, beyond medical procedures, the journey of IVF encompasses a range of emotions, resilience, and human experiences that won't change regardless of any technological advancements.

My quest for the right doctor was driven by a belief in self-advocacy, a theme central to my journey. Advocating for oneself, trusting instincts, and honoring personal feelings are crucial elements in navigating this path. It's about finding what resonates with you as an individual and as a patient.

I hope to inspire introspection, empathy, and a sense of connection through my story and amidst our shared experiences.

Thank you for joining me on this literary journey.

About the Author

Mandy Refvik is a dynamic entrepreneur and inventor whose journey is marked by groundbreaking innovation and a commitment to empowering others. Alongside her husband, she spearheaded the development of the revolutionary healthcare app, "The SugarCube", which stands as a testament to her dedication to integrating cutting-edge technology into the global healthcare landscape.

Driven by her passion for the arts, Mandy ventured into the world of television and film, taking on directing and production roles across various projects in Los Angeles, CA. Her creative endeavors not only showcase her versatility but also underscore her relentless pursuit of excellence in diverse fields.

Beyond her technological and creative ventures, Mandy is deeply invested in supporting women entrepreneurs. Through her active participation on multiple boards, she champions the cause of women in the realms of Web 3.0 and small businesses, embodying a spirit of mentorship and empowerment.

In her personal life, Mandy finds joy in the simple pleasures of shopping and traveling, while also indulging in pursuits such as writing, reading, and exercise. However, her greatest source of fulfillment lies in nurturing her relationship with her daughter, where she imparts valuable life lessons born from her own experiences.

Mandy Refvik's multifaceted career and personal interests epitomize her unwavering commitment to innovation, creativity, and empowerment.

Her journey serves as an inspiration to all aspiring entrepreneurs and advocates for positive change.

Acknowledgments

To every individual who has touched my journey, I extend my sincerest appreciation and admiration.

To my loving and supportive husband Johnnie, my rock who has kept me grounded through all the ups and downs. You always find a way to make me laugh when all I want to do is cry. Your unwavering support and endless love mean the world to me. You are my everything, and I am so grateful to have found my soul mate.

To my parents, Betty and Amerish, your unwavering emotional support and love throughout our journey have meant everything to us. Your example of what true family means has shaped our understanding of love, resilience, and the power of support. Thank you for being our pillars of strength.

To my cherished siblings, Robin, Lynette, Kristofer, Rion, Melissa, and Erik, you are the "anchors" in our lives. Your unwavering encouragement and steadfast presence have been the bedrock upon which I've built my dreams. Your belief in us as individuals and as a couple has been a beacon of light.

To Aunty Deanne, who has been a supporter of our journey and who listened to my long-winded stories, laughing with me and at me. Thank you for being my on-call therapist.

To Onisha, your persistence and positivity have been nothing short of extraordinary. Your unwavering faith in my abilities has propelled me through stormy seas, teaching me that resilience is not just a trait but a way of life.

To Christy, thank you for having that lending ear to my late-night rants when I needed to vent. You always found time for me.

To John and Stephanie, your friendship has been a treasure beyond measure. Your unwavering support and understanding have been a lifeline in moments of doubt, showing me that true friendship is a sanctuary where we find solace, strength, and boundless love.

To Jimmy and Nandini, your infectious laughter and playful banter have been a constant reminder of life's joys. Your ability to find humor in the everyday challenges has been a gift, reminding us of all to never take ourselves too seriously.

To Silvano, your quiet strength and unwavering loyalty have been a source of comfort and reassurance. Your presence has taught us the invaluable lesson that true friendship transcends words, rooted deep in mutual respect and unwavering support.

And to James, though you may no longer walk among us, your spirit lives on in the memories we cherish. Your encouragement, understanding, and late-night conversations will forever echo in our hearts, a testament to the depth of our bond and the impact of meaningful connections.

I am also deeply grateful to the professional team at Barbados Fertility Center, whose expertise and care have been instrumental to our journey. To Dionne Holmes, your unwavering support has been a constant source of strength and inspiration. A true friendship was built on this.

To my OB, Dr. Christy McAvoy, your compassionate care, and expertise have guided me with grace and reassurance, ensuring the well-being of both body and soul.

A heartfelt thanks to my editor, Deanna Novak of The Write Journeys, whose meticulous attention to detail and invaluable feedback have elevated this book to new heights. Your expertise and dedication have left an indelible mark on these pages.